Hope
LOVE &
MIRACLES
STORIES OF THE POWER OF
GOD'S DIVINE HEALING

❖

DR. ELENA BASCOM
and the members of Christian Crossroads Ministry

WELSTAR MEDIA
NEW YORK

Written by Dr. Elena Bascom.
Published by Welstarmedia, LLC.
Horace Batson, PhD., Publisher
628 Lexington Avenue, Brooklyn, NY 11221.
Phone: (646) 409-0340

E-mail:drbatson@optonline.net

ISBN: 978-0-938503-14-9

Managing Editor, Dr.Laura Koplewitz
Book Design/Typography,
Cover Design,

Dedication

Where no counsel is, the people fall:
But in the multitude of counsel there is safety.

PROVERBS 11:14

ॐ

Table of Contents

Foreword

Over the past years the world has experienced devastation in which more than 300,000 people have died as a result of the wrath of the pandemic,COVID-19. In addition to the loss of lives, jobs, and the reshuffling of America's priorities we have had 4 years of an unpresidential Presidency which further fueled hate and dissension among the populace. Thought leaders, doctors and healthcare czars are all baffled and confused. The quest for a cure in the form of a vaccine has just emerged. A vaccine is not enough...

What is woefully needed is a Miracle.

Here in Dr. Elena Bascom's, book - Hope, Love and Miracles: Stories of the Power of God's Divine Healing - we hear the accounts of members of Dr. Bascom's Christian Crossroads church, who by the grace of God, experienced Miraculous intervention. These brave individuals have come forth to share their courageous and inspiring stories.

As publisher for Welstarmedia it has been an honor to bring these incredible stories to light.

Horace Batson, Ph.D.
Publisher, Welstarmedia, LLC.

About The Author
DR. ELENA STERLING BASCOM

Dr. Bascom was born stillborn in Colon, Republic of Panama on February 7, 1945. Shortly thereafter, at the request of her father, she was removed from the trash and came forth screaming. Elena Bascom grew up the eldest of twelve children in a single parent home. At an early age, she embraced her gift to help by assisting her mother with her siblings whenever possible. Despite hunger, homelessness and molestation, Elena completed high school and continued to help her family as she sought a better life.

At the age of twenty-fie, Ms. Sterling left her birthplace with only three hundred dollars and migrated to the United States. Upon her arrival in New York City, she met and married Mr. George Bascom. Out of their union came a son, Edward A. Bascom. Unfortunately, within a short space of time, mental and physical abuse caused the marriage to deteriorate. In the midst of her disappointment and despair over the divorce, Elena persevered, She continued to work while raising her son as a single mother.

At or around Thanksgiving of 1976, Elena Bascom got on the road towards her destiny. Ms. Bascom began her service to God in her community church. She hosted prayer meetings and counseled women with similar experience out of her home. As her ministry began to grow she realized that she needed to further her education. Ms. Bascom went on to receive her doctorate in Theology in 1993. Simultaneously, Christian Crossroads was birthed. Through the ministry, many people who were sick have been healed, lives have been changed, battered individuals have found shelter and families that were broken have been restored.

Rev. Dr. Elena Bascom continues her mission of bringing healing and restoration to families. Dr. Bascom has instituted and facilitated several community outreach programs to support this mission: The Women's Support group, Jericho Road Food Program, Today's Youth, Tomorrow's Leaders, Scholarship Fund, The better Way Literacy Project and the Winner's Circle. Now in the midst of the COVID-19 pandemic the mission continues online…

Hope
LOVE &
MIRACLES
STORIES OF THE POWER OF
GOD'S DIVINE HEALING

✵

DR. ELENA BASCOM
and the members of Christian Crossroads Ministry

WELSTAR MEDIA
NEW YORK

CHAPTER I

Dr. Bascom

FORGIVENESS

❄

Then said Jesus, Father, forgive them; for they know not what they do. (Luke 23:34)

1. Forgiveness is an open gift from God to the world.

2. Love and Forgiveness is the greatest demonstration of God's love from the Cross to man.

3. Forgiveness and love walk together. Without forgiveness love will die. (John 3:16)

4. Forgiveness is a two-edged sword. Forgiveness heals the victim and would extend an opportunity of forgiveness to the criminal. (Hebrew 4:12)

5. Forgiveness brings down the walls and replaces it with a bridge to get us a cross.

6. Forgiveness heals the body and soul. (Matthew 9:2); (Psalms 103)

7. Forgiveness will bring peace to an angry, bitter and tormented soul.

8. Forgive yourself to stop the bleeding, the pain, and start the healing

9. Forgiveness opens closed doors and restores relationship with family and friends.

10. Forgiveness leads you out of darkness into his marvelous light.

11. Forgiveness comes with a commandment and a promise of healing. If we don't forgive those who have trespassed against us, neither will your God forgive your trespasses. (Matthew 6:14-15).

12. I must forgive you, so that I can live.

I am the way, the truth, and the life: no man cometh unto the Father, but by me. (John 14:6)

Praise and worship are weapons against the enemy. When the praises go up the blessings come down.

God is a Spirit and they that worship Him must worship Him in Spirit and in truth. (John 4:23)

We are Sanctified through thy truth. Thy word is truth (John 17:17). Truth is power.

- We should obey the truth
- Declare the truth

- Walk in truth
- Face the truth about yourself and you should bear fruit in the Kingdom of God
- Joy is love strength
- Peace is love security
- God has the last word

The wages of sin is death; but the gift of God is eternal like through Jesus Christ our Lord. (Romans 6:23)

- Sins brings death
- Sin is nonsense
- Sin corrupts good character
- Sin is disobedience of God's Law
- Sin is a lie. A lie is false evidence appearing real. Evil is based on a lie (Evil-Live)
- The Blood, Word, and Spirit bear witness how God works on this earth.
- But without faith it is impossible to please him: for he that cometh to God must believe that he is, and that he is a rewarder of them that diligently seek him. (Hebrews 11:6)
- But that no man is justified by the law in the sight of God, it is evident: for, the just shall live by faith. (Galatians 3:11)

For I have loved thee with an everlasting love: therefore, with loving kindness have I drawn thee. (Jeremiah 31:3)

- The power of love is forgiveness
- God's love will make away
- He's water to the thirsty
- Hope to the hopeless
- Healer to the sick
- Friend to the friendless
- Shelter to the homeless
- Food for the hungry
- Strength to the weak

Many are the afflictions of the righteous: but the Lord deliver him out of them all. (Psalms 34:19)

- Love doesn't abuse or use, love cares and shares.

For the Lord giveth wisdom: out of his mouth cometh knowledge and understanding. (Proverbs 4:7)

- Love is a prescription for your condition. Love doesn't impose, it exposes. Love doesn't make demands it gives you a choice. The love of God looks past your faults and sees your needs.

For with God nothing shall be impossible. (Luke 1:37)

- Joy is love strength
- Gentleness is love conduct
- Face the truth about yourself
- Faith is love confidence

The believer must become love inspired, love mastered, and love driven. Without the fruit of the spirit, we are just religious noise.

- *From the rising of the sun until the going down of the same, the Lord's name is to be praised. (Psalms 113:3)*
- *For his merciful kindness is great towards us : and the truth of the Lord endures forever, praise Ye the Lord. (Psalms 117:2)*
- *The Lord bless thee, and keep thee: the Lord make his face to shine upon me and be gracious unto thee: the Lord lift up his countenance unto thee, and give thee peace. (Numbers 6: 24)*

CHAPTER II

Ms. Dara Sheffield

MIRACLE

--- ❄ ---

In May of 2005 I was blessed to meet Pastor Bascom. During this time I was suffering from depression and anxiety and was taking medication. I was in a very dark place. In my heart and spirit, I could not see my way forward. You never really know that you are down so low, until you are offered a 'hand to stand." My hand to stand and regain my place in the light of the Lord, was Pastor Bascom.

I was on the phone with my cousin, and I let her know just how low I was feeling. Well, she was attending Pastor Bascom's church at the time. Church was not in my thoughts. And then my cousin said "You need to meet my Pastor, you should come to church on this Sunday."

I accepted the invitation, at this point I was willing to try anything to stop the crying every day and the pain I was feeling. That was Saturday, when I talked with my cousin.

As I sat there in my living room, I began to meditate on my past my poor choices and relationships. And then I heard a voice inside my mind, tempting me. It said, "Just kill yourself, nobody cares. Nobody loves you. They won't miss you.

I couldn't believe what I was hearing. This voice in my head — it felt all too real and it was so loud! It completely took over my inner thoughts.

And it was so overpowering, that I began to think of ways that would not be devastating to my three children to find their Mom. You know, you hear that if a person gets real specific about what to do - that is a danger sign.

Well, I got very specific.

I decided to go in my sleep, take some pills that were prescribed to me. As I got up to walk to the bathroom my six-year-old son rang the bell.

I went to answer the door, when I opened the door he almost knocked me down.

My little son, he ran right into my arms, and he yelled "Mommy, I love you!"

So that was the end of that. My Saturday looked different at that point. My plan got put off that day.

I didn't get to the bathroom to take the pills.

I truly thank God for that. I know He used my son to save my life that night

I know that God interrupted the plan of the devil for me

to take my own life.

God used my son that night to save my life and to save my Soul.

I went to Church the next day. It couldn't hurt. I went because my cousin had suggested it. Yet, as I sat through the service, I was feeling like, "What am I doing here?"

Then something extraordinary happened, right at that moment.

Pastor Bascom began to walk down the aisle. She pointed and motioned for me to come up front. I will never forget that day, as I approached tears started to roll down my eyes.

She said to me, "You don't want live!"

That was just so powerful to me! Nobody knew I wanted to take my life the night before but God, me and the devil. I stood there in awe! In that very moment I felt that God really knew me and used a stranger to tell me how I was feeling.

She said to me, "You don't want to live."

Pastor Bascom looked into my soul. She had God with her, looking at me.

And she said "Give your life to God!"

And I did, I received Jesus Christ as the Lord and Savior of my life. Pastor Bascom began to pray for me and my children. The very next day, I woke up feeling like a new woman! I felt life was worth living! And, by the way I never had to take any medication again.

God truly used her to save my life! I am truly grateful!

Miracles don't just stop at one. The Lord has His Ways. And Pastor Bascom is truly one of his Angels here on Earth.

God used Pastor Bascom to perform another miracle with me, soon after. The next miracle was going back to school. The last thing I would ever have thought of doing was to go back to school. I was a single Mom of three children at the time they were 6, 12, and 17. I was receiving public assistance, Honestly, I didn't think I was smart enough to go back to school and complete a degree.

Pastor Bascom prayed for me and encouraged me that I would go back to school and complete my degree. I graduated with two degrees, Associates and Bachelor degree!

To God be the glory! Pastor's prayers gave me faith and hope in God and in myself!! I would not be where I am today, living the life I am living. I remember having some trouble in a math course and Pastor prayed that God would give me a photographic memory and retaining power. God did it I received a B in that class.

It was truly a miracle - not only to be in school, but to go forth and to prosper and be well. With the prayers of Pastor Bascom and God leaning in, I made the college President's List and the Dean's List.

As a single mom, three kids and I was working part time, it was really hard to stay focus with all my responsibilities. But I know it was God who gave me the strength to not quit.

I owe it all to God and to my Pastor for her continual

prayers and encouragement!

I got my two degrees, my A.S., and my BBA. from Monroe College. Just think of it. An A.A. takes a whole two years, and a BBA takes four years,. I earned both in four years.

And lo and behold -- Pastor Bascom prayed for me to get a job there, right at my college. Amazing! This was just what I needed! I interviewed for a part time position as a Administrative Assistant and I got the job on the first interview!!

I was offered the job!! And so while I was in college taking the courses, I started as part time. Then I became full time employee!

Praise be to God! I am now the Director of the Department. To God be the Glory! I was told, you have to have a Masters degree to get the position. But God opened a door and gave me favor! God showed me with trust and faith in him the impossible can be possible.

I could never forget his servant, Pastor Bascom, who interceded for me in prayer. God showed me I didn't need a hand out I needed a way out!

God provided a way through education and a full-time job. I no longer needed subsidy to pay my rent. God made a way for me! And my children — they can see how happy I am and what God has bestowed upon our family. They know we have been blessed.

This next Miracle blew my mind! I was living in an

apartment with no heat for some months. You can imagine Summer you can be fine, then even in Autumn you can put on a sweater. But in Winter? No heat is not possible. I began to pray to God about the situation that was so unbearable.

At the beginning of the year, I was freezing, my family was freezing. You can call the landlord, you can say ' I need heat.' But another path may be your way, if it is God's Way.

Pastor Bascom ministered to me that I needed to move.

This confirmed that God heard my prayer. I had been praying, telling the Lord, I just can't stand this apartment. The landlady wasn't taking care of the repairs, she was always out of the country. She never made any repairs, it was just a mess, a real nightmare.

I'll never forget it, Pastor said to me, "You have to start looking for a place." She didn't say ' Oh just sit tight and hope for the best." That is not God's way. She said I had to act. And through her prayers, God gave me the strength.

Although I was working, I knew I would need money to move. I was thinking to myself where would I get this money from. To move you need at least $6,000-$7,000. It seemed impossible. But I was determined to trust God. If He said it He will make it happen. I felt a little crazy but I said, "Lord, you know what the situation is, so if you want me to move, you're going to take care of it."

Meanwhile Pastor Bascom had no idea that I had no money to move.

Then Pastor ministered to me in the church service one night, and she said, :You need money to move!" I was shocked, Then Pastor prayed that God would make provision for me to move. She prayed and continued to pray that God would make a way.

On a Friday night service she said, "You're going to know the apartment when you see it. It will be two bedrooms and two bathrooms."

Before I found the place God made provision. God used two people to give me with the money I needed. The first was a check for $ 4,000 and the second was $2,000. I was so overwhelmed with joy, God did it. I now had what I needed to move. Every time I think about it, tears fill my eyes! What a blessing! God paid it all. Moving expenses and all. I didn't have to owe anyone a dime!

Praise Be to God! I surely did find the apartment with two bedrooms and two bathrooms, exactly as God had said. It was located across the street from one of the brothers in the church. Look at God! He gave me favor with the realtor, and the landlady.

As I look back, I thank God for His mercy, grace and favor. I thank God for bringing me to CCM. I thank God for Pastor Bascom. She has been truly a blessing to me and my family! I'm beyond grateful for her service, sacrifice and dedication to seeing God's will performed in our lives.

CHAPTER III

Mr. Edward Bascom

MIRACLE

* * *

I joined the military and as everybody knows, there are many situations an individual in the Afmed Forces can face in which you do not know if that final outcome in a military action – what it is. Will it be that you survive - or not. It is what you sign up for – protecting our country, and you learn skills that help with stepping up to the moment, whatever risk is called for. Without a doubt, it helps tremendously being a person of great faith. Praying to Our Lord is never more real than if you are out and deployed. For, in my heart I knew He had my back.

The situations that happen bring in the military, you just cannot know what will be your challenge, and what God will inspire in you. For just as He watches over His Children, there is a role that is inspired by Him. In all walks of Life, I have discovered that the Lord is the great protector. I know that He is with me. For, he makes himself known!

If you think that our Lord just stays in the background – no! He makes Himself really known! There is no mistaking miracles — when it happens you know for sure it is His Divine intervention.

There have been many miracles prior to my entering the military. But the most profound miracles have been when I've been on my own and I had to experience life for myself in the military.

So there are many examples. Let me tell you the first one – it is a two part series. Being in the military, when I signed up, I will let you know it was the first time that I ever been alone by myself without any family members. At some time in each of our lives we will be apart from family.It is also in the military when you are suddenly called upon to have extreme discipline. The military tells you when to rise, what to wear, how to salute, how to turn, how to address your officers, going through basic training you do not have a moment in which you are going to be fully free to just schedule your time yourself. The schedule is a shock! It can be very good the structure and also -- a shock! You cannot watch movie, put your feet up, have a home-cooked meal, lounge around for an evening. You do not have time and you are not allowed. All that familiarity drops away, and the people you know and who know you — and that comfort of loved ones — you are completely without that. You are truly on your own.

And that in itself was a traumatizing experience. And also the fact that in the military, it is not your neighborhood. You do not know who is next to you in the barracks, or who you have to work with on a task, who you get teamed up with. It is all of America --the whole melting pot. Imagine every person from every neighborhood across the country, all the different stripes of people, and that is who I was seeing, and interacting with. I had to learn how to be open to people from city, country, all the races, all the cultures. I was suddenly in a sea of faces and people that I had not been swimming in before. It can be – I'll be candid – it can be traumatizing. You feel you are not in a community in the same way as your neighborhood. You all joined up, you are training together, living together, but you are all very different. It can make you feel alone.

The third traumatizing thing was dealing with military leadership, and them forcing you into another way of lifestyle than the one you are accustomed to living. The top down is a set of rules you agreed to abide by, and you do. You can't say 'No, don't feel like doing that right now.' You chose to serve, but it is not easy to follow orders all the time. You have to keep parts of yourself from rebelling, you have to change. It is very challenging to do.

So there were layers of things – and plus dealing with my own issues, there were layers of things that was just compounded, on what I was experiencing. So it became a very depressing moment for me in my life, and a turning point because if you ever read Joseph Campbell, the story *The Hero's Journey*,this is were I embark on my journey into the unknown. When you start on your journey and you look for all the resources to help you overcome the obstacles in life. So this became for me, in the military, what I call the Joseph Campbell story, *The Hero's Journey.* The Hero doesn't sit at home wondering about life or just watching it go on for others. He doesn't jut read about it or see it on the nightly news. He gets up, he goes out this front door. He leaves home. He starts on his journey, and it takes him to new places and unknown situations, unknown destinations. And for me, joining the military, going out there and facing these trials and tribulations - it was to see how I'd deal with it

And if you are in your journey facing the unknown – you learn about parts of yourself you didn't know about, too. So your voyage out – is a voyage in, as well.

What I discovered is that it was not just 'me' inside myself, and ' other people' out in the world. Lo and behold – it turns out that God is with you – everywhere.

There were many miracles at this juncture. One big change for me was that before the military, I did not know how to meet a difficulty in life. I could not even acknowledge or respond to difficult situations my life. Moreover, prior to this moment, if I experienced something that I didn't like or I couldn't deal with it, I'd just ignore it hoping it would go away. For a number of years as a teen, and as an adult, I choose not to resolve my problems, I just didn't respond to the issues I was dealing with.

An example is: Prior to this moment, like if there was a creditor calling and I owed something, and I didn't pay it, or I couldn't pay it at the time, I would have just not even answered the phone! Or I'd tell them the check is in the mail. I believed, " If you ignore something long enough it will go away."

But after I discovered God in my life, what I found is that the more you ignore something – the bigger the problem grows. I could see what the negative results were, instead of pretending the results were somebody else's fault or my bad luck. I could see it was that I was ignoring problems, and this imperiled me and those around me, my loced ones. It took awhile to change, but with the Lord's help, I began see I had been on a wrong path. It was not a Hero's Journey. Not looking at what was going on in my life was never going to make it go away.

Right. You can't ignore a crisis! It is a crisis! So it was a tremendous learning experience. Because the philosophies that you have and what you look at is not actually how life is. And until you experience it, you will always have these little things – patches – little momentary fixes,that maybe worked for me when I was going through high school or college.

But that's not how the bigger picture of life works. So it's a difficult transition from school to life. When you walk out the door on a quest, you do not leave that behind, those issues you've built up, like debts you want to ignore. You run into them as almost the first thing that happens. To get anywhere on your journey, you have to confront your life issues. You can't even begin, if you are carrying things you don't want to look at — with you.

In school you could ignore the teacher or ignore the grade. Like in college we had a teacher called the dragon lady. And if you come in late, you get an F. If you speak out of turn, you get an F. One day I walked in and got six Fs. So I dropped the class that same day. But I'm saying that was just something where I'd say to myself, "It's no big deal." But you can't do that in life. And so that was the major anxiety, like the things that I used to do I can no longer do anymore, if that makes sense.

The miracle part – is when my life started to change for the better. I'm on this quest, I've walked out the door thinking I'm leaving problems behind me.

And then there were three sets of miracles.

These were God's Wake-Up Calls.

First miracle: Here's what is going on - I'm dealing with depression. Here's what led up to me being very despondent. It a collision between my world of ' just letting things slide by,' and that was a very thin, wall of little excuses and denials I'd stacked up inside. Then real life showed up, and that was military. It was like a truck, carrying a ton of bricks hitting me.

That thin wall inside me of ' Oh I'll get by with little excuses –
well –wow, it crumbled right down. It happened when I went
to my first duty station in Seoul, Korea.

The specific scene was this: While embarking on my first
field training exercise in the military,right on the border with
North Korea, I experienced my first dilemma. The walls inside
of me were tested.

I was assigned to a medical unit, working under the
military Operations Officer. If you picture a country you've
never been to. It is winter. It's cold - really cold. You are not
sure of your surroundings or how the entire country works.
Everything is unfamiliar. The roads. The hills. Nothing is
familiar. And even all the details of who is there with you.
You're under command and you are there following orders.

The military Operations Officer, his role is that he has
command over the training, and he welfare of the soldiers and
the junior officers, too. The Operations Officer is planning
and putting into play troop deployments, weapons systems,
communications in training and in actual combat. This
individual has a wide range of authority and is very pivotal to
troop safety.

In Seoul South Korea, in winter, the Operations Officer
decides to take an action that is tactical and - dangerous. He
believed that being in a medical unit was not being a real
soldier. So, in fact he decided up the stakes on our military
training. Unfortunately, this was always the issue when you

enter into the military, dealing with over zealous commanding authorities, whom sometimes would put a troop action at the forefront – and in doing that - disregard safety.

You are a soldier, and you have no choice but to listen, and follow orders. Thus our Operations Officer wanted to drive up a mountain that had dangerous road conditions, because of snow and inclement weather conditions.

This is the scenario in my life, in which God showed his hand, and I was sue without a doubt that He had my back.

I experienced my first abyss in the middle of the mountains while driving the vehicle for the S-3 cooperations officer. I don't know if you've ever seen a real live abyss. A real live abyss.

And I'm not speaking in a symbol here – this is not a metaphor!. This is the actual thing — an abyss!. It is a straight drop. Nothing there to hold you. That's it. You are gone forever.

I had to drive the Officer up the mountain. So we drove up – I was behind the wheel, that was my duty. There were no guardrails.

No – nothing. So if you can imagine that you're in the mountain and there is a big abyss, and the snow is coming down, which made the driving conditions hazardous.

So I spoke up. I'm telling u superior, "This is not a good idea because coming back down is gonna be a problem." And he says, " No, let's go, let's go, everything is gonna be all right."

But I could tell: No, it's not gonna be all right, because by the time we come back down road conditions are going to be icy.

So we get to the site where we supposed to set up. We are the recon team – it means we were first up -and we checked and cleared the way for the unit. We observed the surroundings and decide that with the current weather conditions it was not safe for the unit to follow.

Well, yet there we were. So now we're coming down the mountain. Now the road conditions are horrible. And now we're next to the abyss. So now, if going up wasn't a problem. Coming down is the problem. So we coming down, and I look, and right now I'm next to the abyss, and I am very uncomfortable with driving next to the abyss.

I'm looking at my commanding Officer. It is obvious the road condition is not safe,

My heart is beating fast, this is not what I wanna do. I thought it would've been better to leave the car up there for a minute and then walk down and get help. That would have been the safest thing to do.

He gets out of the car and says, "I'll direct you." Now I didn't even think, I'm still in the vehicle, and if it if it goes down - he's safe. He's on his feet. He is saying he will direct me. And he is safe. And where am I?

I'm – wow, you know – I am under his command – and I thought maybe his direction would've helped me.

As I'm going down the hill, the car slips. And I don't

know how, I can't explain it, but the car slips, and I touch the edge of that abyss with the car tires. It starts to go over.

Suddenly - I am able to veer the car back to the right side, bring it back from going over, and I come down the hill, without the car slipping.

So I make it down to the bottom of this hill — by myself in the car. And then the Officer, he comes into the car and says, "Bascom, are you all right?"

I just looked at him and I didn't speak. I just didn't speak. It was a taxing moment. "Are you all right?" he repeats. I just didn't speak again. I just kept driving. He is back in the car after I get the car to a safe spot.

I drove down the rest of the mountain in the ice and the snow falling all around. Then I get out. And then my knees are so weak from the anxiety, I fall down.

And so the military, it gave me an impact award for doing that. Now what would an impact award and a badge do for you if you had fallen down the abyss. It wasn't worth a life!

This was my first miracle.

Noe, of course Pastor wasn't there in South Korea with me! I was able to make a phone call the night before and she prayed for my safety and said the 91st Psalm, "He that dwelt in the secret place of The Most High shall abide under the shadow of the Almighty." It is a very powerful prayer especially in your time of need.

Pastor, who is also my mother, not only did she pray for

me the night before I went up the mountain. We prayed in the morning together before I took that ride. The 91st Psalm was our banner form danger and keeper in the midst of darkness.

U was holding onto the belief and praying that I was able to make that tour. Or else I could've been in the abyss, I wouldn't have this conversation and relate this experience. Because it was very real. There's no way that I could really explain it to you. You would have had be there. It was truly terrifying.

It it seemed like a lifetime. 'Cause I looked into the abyss, it was dark, there was nothing there. I didn't even know an abyss existed in this world until I saw it with my own eyes, and I almost slipped in.

Right then, I looked directly into the eternal fall into to a dark abyss

And .Pastor Bascom had protected me with the Lord's prayers. The 91st Psalm surrounded me and kept me from going over.

That's one of the Miracles that changed me. One of them, yeah.

So going along my life's journey, remember I mentioned my story is layered with miracles. And several showed up when I was in the military, on my own. Overall, I was in the military on assignment for nine years. It was like the symbolic Hero's Journey. It is not that you are being heroic - that is not the meaning. You can't just start out doing heroic acts.

The Hero's Journey says that when you start out from home, you will have challenges ahead, in front of you. And only as you meet those and find out what your tests of character are — then you can start learning to be yourself and know about the world. You don't know who you are until you go out in the world and challenges will inevitably come your way. This is not the same as looking for trouble!

I remember reading about the Prodigal Son. At some point, all you want to do is go back home, into the fold. Back to your flock and to safety. You don't want any more trials. Yet you may not have a choice, you have to go on.

Now, after literally almost ending up in the abyss, I know absolutely I was saved by a Miracle, and I know Pastor Bascom and God saved me. I wanted go back home. I wanted to retreat.

I thought — I cannot do this on my own. After experiencing all these different attitudes, having to follow authority even if I felt it is was bad judgment -- I'm saying to myself, ' I don't wanna do it any more.'

But here's the thing in the military, right? In the army they don't really allow you to quit like that!

You cannot just say, "I'm not happy!" Or, ' I don't like this anymore, I want to quit and go home!"

I've seen in basic training, when a person said they were tired and they wanna go home. Well, okay, the officer in charge says, "Sure, we'll let you go home." And then the next thing you doing, is pushups and other strenuous exercises. You are shown what it is like to want to quit. Let's just say it is not an attitude that gets rewarded. Ultimately you change your mind and you convince yourself it is not so bad.

It is a certain psychology. 'Cause you have to go through a whole process to leave. And at som point during that, you realize that it is not worth the the process to leave, and to go through that. It discourages you from leaving. But you still might feel you want to. You don't. Instead, like in any situation where you feel unhappy and you can't leave. If you feel trapped, it is easy to get depressed. You lose a sense of will. You can feel your own destiny is controlled on the outside. It is easy to give up on the inside.

Okay, so let me get to one of the other Miracles.

I became very despondent. And so I was thinking to end it. Because at this point I can't leave. I don't have family members around. Usually I have a support group around and these people arround me at that time, did not seem to understand me. I'm in South Korea, very far away from everybody - friends, family. And I'm having arguments and fights left and right. Because you've gotta rememer, in the military in another country -- one that is next door to a dictator nation. And in a situation that can be tense - you are on edge. You are in training. You could be called into a war situation. You are on your guard.

So you are in high protection for yourself. And it

is natural in that type of situation, people from different backgrounds, and everyone with his own authority, or egos and attitudes. This was the make it or break it point for me and I was entering a dark place in my life seemingly with nothing to lose.

It's like you're entering Gladiator School. The strain of living with people from all walks of life in a make it or break life was not exciting for me — at first. It got better but at first, this was all strange to me.

You are in a foreign country, and among the ranks of your own solders, tensions come out. You could see and feel intolerance among the races in the troops. You had martial arts experts You had to be on your guard. And so as a matter of fact, one day I see my friend, on the way to the chow hall, I encounter two white guys beating up on my Hispanic friend. I speak Spanish and English. I stepped in. I had to stop and help him fight the two guys.

And then Sergeant in charge blamed me for the fight and took me to my instructors. So the instructor indicates to the Sergeant that I was the provocateur, and I started hitting the platoon guys.

Now the guy who brought me in, he had no interest in hearing my story. I am African-American , and there was intolerance and bias behind the situation. The guy who dragged me into the office, he was white. He just assumed I was wrong and he had no interest in hearing my side of the situation. I do think in that situation there was some bias at work. In fact he made up his version - that I had instigated a fight with these two platoon guys.

In reality, I had just come along and tried to help, and I was now in hot water. So I asked my friend to verify and explain to my superiors. Then I asked them if they could give me two minutes to hear what had happened from my perspective.

When I told them the story what actually happened, they were so impressed that I helped one of my fellow platoon guys, that I got off without punishment or being written up. They knew that I was telling the truth.

If I had not tried, and made an effort to communicate, and I'd given up inside and kept myself quiet, it could have been a whole different consequence and a very negative outcome.

Especially if I didn't address the problem right, I would have not been in a situation where truth won out. I would have been at the mercy of a racist person who had assumed I was in the wrong. In earlier years in my life, I would have run away, not faced the challenge. And even in the military, I hsd grown very despondent, So I could have just allowed other people and their negative attitudes to control my life.

I knew I standing in the light of truth - so I stood my ground. I wasn't angry, or belligerent. I just spoke up. I stayed steady. I did not run or blow my top. I just stood there and clearly and calmly spoke ' truth to power.' I don't know how I had the fortitude right then. I was afraid, inside, sure. I thought I would not be heard. But something inside me, that was bigger than my fears, stepped up to the moment. So, I tried anyway. And by speaking up and telling my truth to the authorities — it was the right thing to do. My voice was heard.

I learned that you have to learn how to communicate. Communication is the key to life.

Because if you can't express your thoughts or express what happened in a clear and direct manner, if you do not even try — how can you be heard?

There is a phrase in the Bible- about our Lord. It is about listening for him. In the wind, or in your prayers, or in the silence. You listen and you can hear 'The still, small voice."

That day, I felt the "still small voice" had welled up within me, and gave me the faith and courage to speak up. The Lord had dwelled inside of me.

Our Lord and Savior was giving me a lesson. It was a gift of His voice.

He spoke within me, and I found the courage.

I found a new sense of belief that day. It is that there is a bigger sense than yourself, it is where we are standing in God's eyes. He is looking in upon us, and teaching us that communication helps anyone to acquire the things they may need for their journey. This was my first initiation process in life learning to communicate.

That day, I experienced two different things-- opposites. And I was not yet feeling I had a choice about going up out of darkness and choosing to walk in light. I had stood up for myself, but I was still in a state of despair.

I'm speaking my truth. And yet simulraneously I'm at the lowest point. I don't wanna be here — I mean in a big way. I don't want to be living any more. I don't want to be in the military anymore. I don't want life anymore.

I was then, in my life, struggling with faith. And it was a torment.

So what I did then, is I called my Mom. She is my Mom and my Pastor. And I said to her that I felt I needed to say goodbye. And you may have thought that it was about the military. But when I said it to her, I meant that I wanted to leave life. I was saying goodbye. I wanted to kill myself.

And of course no mother wants to hear her child say this. A mother might at that time have felt helpless with her son so far away and being in such a dark moment in his life.

You have to remember, however, my Mom is also my Pastor.

So my Mom prayed that God would send me wordd of inspiration and speak to me at my point of need. And the next day I went to Sunday service. There are all different kinds of services in the military. The 11:30 A.M. Mass is the English Mass. And it's the Pentecostal Mass.

I walk in. And the Pastor preaches a sermon called "Too

Legit to Quit." I still remember that sermon today. I thought it was just incredible that he started talking about life and why you shouldn't quit. And that helped me that day not to do it- not to quit on my life.

Having that intervention of the Pastor, and my own Pastor, my Mom, who prayed for me, they lifted me out of the dark place I had been in.

I decided through their prayers, and that sermon, that I would stick around. I had wondered what life was worth living for. But God's voice stayed with me, and helped me to hear that "stiill, small voice." Now the thing about it was, that life I did realize, it took time, but I saw that life has so much more meaning than what I was convinced of before that Miraculous time. Prayers lifted my soul up. God's voice whispered inside of me. They went hand in hand and together I was raised up from that dark place in my spirit.

And you would never experience it if you don't live through it to see what's on the other side. Everything is a preparation for you to go to your destination. I was being prepared for a life journey. But because I didn't have a vision, goal, and a life direction, I thought it ended right there. I was taking a temporary situation and making it a permanent destination.

And a lot of people probably just don't see that there's another way, that there's any hope. I was very demoralized. I was also feeling hopeless. A part of me wasn't sure what worth my life had.

Until you experience challenges that make you face yourself, you have done nothing. If I had it to do all over again, I would never do it that way. You don't have to put yourself through dark places and fear and loss of hope. You don't want to do that to yourself.

But if you find yourself there, it is extremely important to realize there is faith, and prayer, and unconditional acceptance of you as a person, by our Lord and Savior. Others who are in an open channel with God, will help you, they will shine God's light into you and search for you even if you want to hide away. You find a way out of your darkness, with God as the guide.

You walk out the door of your home, and you start on your path.

I think I was also under another illusion and God helped me to see my way out of that one, too.

Here is what happened. Hen I went to the recruiter and I signed up for the military, I went in the office for the recruiter to sign up, with my good friend Valentino. He and I had figured, "This is great, we'll be in this together."

We signed up and we wanted to go to Panama together, we were supposed to be stationed together, or so we had hoped. E both were sure we'd be going to Panama together, and we could help each other through getting to know how to be in the military. I was sure we'd do that together - or I wouldn't have even signed up.

I figured when I was assigned a separate basic training, that when we got through the first part, he was gonna meet me in the second part. He never came. We signed up together on the hope that we'd be stationed together. We thought it worked that way. And nobody said we couldn't be choosing to be stationed together — so it was a little of a ' bait and switch'… !

I survived, and I survived the military but mostly I survived my own doubts and I survived my own former self. And I learned and grew. Here I am — home again. But I'm not home because I ran home out of fear. I chose to come back, this too, is part of my journey. I am alive, and helping your Mom with the ministry.

And with Pastor Bascom, miracles are coming out left and right. They never stop at my Mom's church. They never stop.

We dedicated our lives to helping people. And so that's what we do.

Lest I skip over another very important miracle in my story, my third major miracle was when I was still in the military, and I was becoming promotable and I needed to go Non-Commissioned Officers Academy in order to remain eligible for promotion.

I failed on my first attempt going to the NCO Academy and it was traumatizing. They made us run in the middle of the day when the sun is at its apex the grueling heat got the best of me. And I failed my run by only ten seconds. I missed my qualification by 10 seconds.

There's a qualification time that you have. So normally I run two miles at 14:30. That day I ran it in 16:30. And I needed to run it in 16:20. So I missed it by 10 seconds.

he problem is, is when you fail an NCOS school, they don't send you back. Yeah, that's right. Your career is done. It stops there, no promotion eligibility.

The command doesn't send up for the training people that they think are going to fail. I was in the qualifying stage and I failed that run by 10 seconds.

Imagine you are the Commander making the decisions. You don't know me, but you're just looking at the record. You say to yourself, "OK, he failed. I'm not sending him forward for the training. I've got other soldiers that need that to get promoted. So If you're the Commander, you put me to the side.

And you have to make a command decision. you don't want to send someone with a bad record, completion is a must. And remember, it's all about looking good on their evaluation and making command decisions. So why would I, as Commander, send a soldier that already failed?

Remember you're in charge of a big budget and a command decision.

But in my position, I'm eligible for moving up in the ranks, and if you stay at the same rank, more than a certain amount of time you're done. So they said my officer career was over, it would not happen.

And so my mother prayed. She said, "delay is not denial, Failure is not written in stone, and I do not care what anyone says, God is gonna take you through."

And everybody was telling her "Your son he's not going to get a second chance to go back, they do not send people back a second time."

"My son is going back to the command." My mother prayed. And she sat down with me. And had to tell her, "Ma, I don't think this is gonna happen."

So at this point I'm trying to be realistic, and take it for what it is. I did not succeed at that qualification run. Period.

Anyway,it came time for me to reenlist. The miltary asked me, are you going to reenlist. It was at that point a choice I could make. Ye or no. Re-enlist or leave the military.

I stood up for myself. I said, "I've gotta go to the training school first."

Now this is not supposed to happen but the military sent me back for a second try! They sent me back -- they put in a request for me to go back to the school. When I got to the school, my eyes had a problem all of a sudden. My eyes started to swell, I could not see. I'm sick, and I can not go on with the training. It meant that I could not go back and all is lost. Whatever it is, I can't go back. This is your life on steroids. That's it. Your only shot. I go to the military doctor's office. If they diagnose my eye with a sty, I'm going back home.

My eyes were like two big balloons. I couldn't see. So in order to hear the marching orders, and keep in step, I'm gonna have to listen to when the guys say left, left, right. That's how I was walking. I couldn't see.

Anyway, I get there to the military doctor's office, and I couldn't see. And a guy gets a sty in there too. It looks about to be that I am going to be considered the cause of that!

But when the doctor diagnosed me, he said it's not a sty. My eyes just blew up from going to the contrasts of cold, heat, or whatever. So the class is only four weeks. The second week now my eye begins to come down.

I am slowly getting in the clear. But not yet!

And now I face my next greatest challenge, which is land navigation. Land navigation is where you have to use a compass and find your points on a map. Anyway, I did that. I found the five spots. And I became a Sergeant.

I the Miracle was that I got in at all into the training school! I was off the list. Then my Mom, who is my Pastor, prayed. I shouldn't have been in the program at all. That's it. My career was done.

My career was not done. I went forward. I passed and got a promotion.

My Pastor, who is also my Mom, has prayed for me right through the journey I have been on. And now, I am back home, and the Miracles never cease. I am right where

I want to be. The military part of my journey is behind me. The life lessons I learned, and God's "still, small voice " those are inside of me, with my Mom's prayers, the Lord is with me now and always. When I stand up, the Lord stands within me, and when I am in danger, or at risk of failing, I am lifted up. I thank the Lord and my Pastor Bascom, my mother, for walking me towards the light that is inside me. I know that light is in us all.

Ask yourself: What if you encounter an issue that really requires your attention, not just a quick fix? For example what if you need to protect others and you have always run away from the littlest difficulty? You will not be up for the task. You will miss your mark at that moment.

Then you learn in life's challenges, standing up and taking courage, is not just about you.

And that is what I started learning from the Lord, through His Miracles.

He started helping me see life more clearly. And this was through Pastor that I experienced the power of God's intervention. It was not just for me, I realized. It was for those who feel imperiled, whether from outer dangers or inner demons.

Strength came from the Lord and from my Pastor's prayers. I was fighting with self doubt, and feeling that I had no voice, that I could not be heard. I felt I was lost and did not know my way.

The Lord and Pastor Bascom helped me to start understanding more about how when you walk with the Lord - you change. Life changes.

And I say "life," - and not just "my life." Because what the Lord's guiding hand and Pastor's prayers have been teaching me is - It is not just 'your life's journey you are on.

We are not one by one walking alone. We are together in God's eyes.

Do you notice we are called "God's Children." Jesus is the Lord's Son.

The rest of us too: we are God's Children. That means all of us. Even in your darkest hour, that means you.

So I'd say listen for the "still, small voice." Know that as His Voice .

Is heard inside of you - so too, will you hear your own.

That's at least three Miracles - and I'm still counting all the others!

CHAPTER IV

Ms. Emily LaBorde

MIRACLE

---　❁　---

I am a social worker, and I love my work. It is certainly
at times challenging, but what really matters are the people I
help. I've worked in foster care, that was a good experience. I
worked with youth sexual offenders, they have tough problems
and issues. I worked for Community Based Organization
that were contracted with the DOE to provided mental
health services to Jr HS and HS students who were serving
a superintendent suspension for various infractions. Young
people are in great despair, and I love working with them and
their families.

Helping people is important to me. There are many
people in the world who need healing and if you can help,
then it is definitely good to do that. Currently I'm working as a
School Social Worker. Well, I'll mention that I'm pretty happy

about this, because actually, I've been trying to get a job as a school social worker.

How do you know whether what you are doing in your life is meaningful? Do you know if you'll help others? What are the best reasons to do a certain job? How do you know if your job is right? Are there ways to know?

Goals may seem like something that you just arbitrarily decide, and then you see what happens. Setting goals in life can make a person feel good. But the times when it doesn't really work out can be disappointing. When I graduated from NYU it was hard for me to become a school social worker in NYC. Applying is a long process, and admittedly, even when I did figure it out, it was almost impossible to get a response from a school's Principal to get an interview.

There are often times in life when a personal goal is very important, and finding meaningful work for me, is extremely important.

So one day we were in church and I mentioned to Pastor Bascom, that there was an opening in the Board of Ed. I know that talking about a job in church may seem like it is not very important. I mentioned to my Pastor, the job was in a different department, not a school social worker position. Pastor Bascom encouraged me to apply for it, which I did.

It can be very surprising, when a very practical aspect of life, such as a job, and your church and Pastor, connect in your life. It mattered to me so very much that my Pastor had the intuition that I should apply because I knew that God uses her and I had to seek wise counseling. I was not thinking that was what I should do. I'd ruled that out because it wasn't in the department I had want to work in. Yet you can think you know your path, and rule out other options because you don't want to make mistakes in life and want to walk the path God has for you.

My Pastor helped me. She said to me, let's trust God.

There are ways that Pastor Bascom understands a person - at times better than you understand yourself. That is truly the connection with the Lord. If your Pastor sees into you and sees what will help you-- you can do nothing better than to listen. I listened to her advice. I knew that God was going to do something and my Pastor held my hand and prayed when my faith got low.

Because, faith is a tough thing. You may think, when it is offered to you, ' No, this is not for me. What if I have faith for it to happen -- and it doesn't! What If I hope? And then -- what if faith fails? Isn't that even worse than not having faith?

Yet, when there is a calling -- and a whisper -- and it is from your Pastor, then there is reason to let go and let God. Because-- your Pastor has the gift from God and you can take heart to what she says.

And so I did. I applied for the job. It was not directly what I thought I'd be eligible for, but Pastor Bascom said - ' Go ahead -- apply.' And this made all the difference to me.

Thanks be to God — and to Pastor Bascom. And in the words of poet Robert Frost, I truly did take the ' road less traveled' and it has changed my life all for the better.

I was hired and that position was truly a blessing. It was about a year or close to a year ago, and one day in church, Pastor said to me, "I don't know why, but you're gonna be working in another department and I could see you going from school to school."

I started to question what position this was because I never heard of a job that would require someone to go from school to school. God would lead Pastor to pray for me from time to time. She would continue praying, by saying, "I could see you going from school to school" and one day she added, "And you're gonna get hired on the spot".

Months later God opened another door this time, for a school Social Worker position. I did meet some obstacles but truly God saw me through. I was called in for an interview and met with the Principal and the Assistant Principal and literally what Pastor for prayed, and what she saw in the future-- this is exactly what happened. Praise Be to God!! One never knows how God can use people and how much he loves us and he can bless you. And then he led me to the job that I had truly longed for!!

I found out that I would be the School Social Worker for 3 schools and I would be going from school to school. The interview was short and they called the School Psychologist to come downstairs. When she came into the room they asked her to show me to my new office!

Wow. I was looking at the Principal and the Assistant Principal, and then there was the School Psychologist in front of me. In my physical presence — I was there with them. And in my heart, in my spirit - I thanked God. And I knew that Pastor Bascom was used by God. She knew with such strength of conviction — that God was using her to help me.

The job I had truly hoped for - was offered to me.

Exactly what Pastor Bascom had prayed - that is exactly what happened. It was perfect, it literally was a miracle, 'cause something that I tried to do since 2001 something I've tried to do for 17 years! — God literally did this within less than a year.

When your Pastor approaches you with the gift of prophecy and her prayer, honestly, in her interaction with me – there was no big announcement in advance! God truly works in mysterious ways. It's almost like you don't know when the Lord is coming. But for Pastor Bascom — she felt a certain ' knowing' and there was no hesitation. In a very direct way - she simply said, ' Apply - and this job will be offered to you on the spot.' God has this way of using her to reach out to us and she makes herself available.

There is not a way to ' plan' and say ' I will do this and it will then lead to that.' Not with a miracle – it is truly spontaneous, and yet it is part of God's plan. And my Pastor was the conduit. She was the channel for the Lord to wake me up. I was encouraged to trust God and hold onto my faith.

God would give us instructions and He offered Pastor Bascom the gift of helping me to know my path – in God's mighty way. Pastor Bascom confirmed to me, that God created this social work position for me.I did not know they were clustering School Social Workers and assigning them to more than one school.

How God works is truly a blessing and a miracle. What exactly a person does each day, can lead to misery, for oneself and others, or to fulfillment and happiness. When one is doing the Lord's work – this is truly a blessing.

I had hoped to be in a role as a School Social Worker. The Social Workers are different from Guidance Counselors, who provide more of the at-risk student counseling, and the support for graduating students. And that is such an important help for students.

But my role – it is different. I have to go into the spirit and the heart of what is happening in a student's life — in his or her entire world, in a sense. I have to do evaluations for children whose parents request a special education evaluation. I meet with parents and explains the special education process, informs them of their due process rights and conduct observations and evaluations that contribute to the special education process.

Often times, parents may be confused. They may be upset and anxious, and not knowing what will become of their children in the school system. They want to protect their children. And if this is a special education evaluation — the parents are afraid. Will their children get what they need in school? So, they are turning to me for more than they may even know. They are turning to me for information, and also – reassurance. I know that when I help them, and their children, I hope to bring them reassurance, and help them with a pathway forward.

My Pastor Bascom actually helped me to see – that if you are helped to find your path, you also learn courage – you learn strength. You then take that strength, and you help others to find their own. So for the parents, and the kids, my goal is to help with the concrete details they need to know. And my other goal is to help them to feel reassured.

This all goes back to Dr Bascom. This is how Dr. Bascom works wonders. And with her own intuitions and prayers – well - this is how the Lord helps her, too. For Dr. Bascom is a gift from God and she helps people – to help others – and that is the way all of us find help — it is a love — and a healing that goes on – and on.

Well, work is one sphere in how God used Dr. Bascom to help me. But it is not the only way she helped and brought me to the Lord, and brought the Lord to me, through her guidance.

I have two children. I came to church single, living out of my parents' home. And when I got saved in 2003, that was a miracle because I was not church-going at all, l nor were my parents. My parents were doing a lot of things when it came to who they believed in, worshipped and what practices they were engaging and at one point not believing in Jesus. So, actually, prayer and believing in God and Jesus was actually forbidden to me and my siblings to even say things like "God Bless you" when someone sneezes" or anything of that sort. That was how I lived my life, no Jesus, no God.

One of my roommates in college who is a dear friend to me still to this day would pray every morning and every night very quietly to herself and I would watch her then turn my back and say under my breath…."yeah right not me". She was only my roommate for our freshman year in college and went back home after our first semester ended.

There was a time in my life that I hit a very low point and I was in my room crying, I heard in my spirit, "Jesus". And I heard it three times. And on the third time I cried and called upon the name Jesus.

And it must have been calling out in my spirit because at that time my parents were home, my sister was home, her boyfriend was home, the dog was there. No one came to my room to check on me.

But I basically called my friend who was my roommate the first semester of freshman year and told her I want to go to church. And yeah that was in 2003. She was an open door to God for me, I got saved, I was as surprised as anybody.

And I haven't stopped going since.

And that was Christian Crossroads Ministries, and Dr. Elaine Bascom was the Pastor.

So that in and of itself is just one of those moments that shows how God is just so awesome and knows your future and what you need in life.

Ever since I started coming I have witnessed how God is able to help his people and how He uses Pastor Bascom in a very, very particular way. And since I've been in church, I got a job paying a very reasonable salary, I got married in the church, my husband's family and my in-laws are there. We conceived our two children in the church. They were both christened in the church and they were both baptized in the church.

There is nothing more miraculous than when the Lord intervenes on behalf of your children.

My son he is truly a miracle from God.

One day in service Pastor called me up and she said, "I don't know why, but God said to take communion during your pregnancy."

I recently had found out that my husband and I were expecting our first child. So when Pastor ministered to me I was thinking, "okay". I did not understand especially why Pastor Bascom had called - but I know she was guided -- what she knew is that this is what she had to say to me.

We did not know what God was doing but He used Pastor to give me these instructions to take communion every day during the pregnancy, so I did. I got my 'take home communion kit.' And the Pastor prayed over the box of communion and every morning I would take one.

One day I had an appointment to go for a routine sonogram. Pastor did not know about the appointment but she called me up for prayer in service and said something like this, "anything that you receive, if you don't want it, you're gonna reject it, don't receive it" and said "the only report you believe is the report of the Lord, and that report from the Lord, is saying that everything is well."

And I said, "Okay. "And I wasn't really thinking anything of it. That is -- until I went to the sonogram appointment. The technician was doing the sonogram, and after, I learned that the baby was showing a cyst on his kidney. He explained to me that usually it grows, or it stays there, but he needs to monitor it because if it grows, we have to start looking at what our next step is.

I did not know what that meant. But I said"All right".

I got off the table. I got dressed and as I was walking through the hallway it came right back into my mind what I should do:

I said to myself, "I reject the doctor's report and the only report I will receive in my heart, is the report of the Lord over my son," that all is well.

I came to church and I told the Pastor about it and she prayed. Pastor continuously prayed about this situation and I continued to take communion.

A couple of months later I had my follow up appointment to assess the cyst that was on my son's kidney. This time it was another technician doing the sonogram.

She was looking at my chart, and at the same she's looking at the sonogram screen and she kept on doing this. She then asked me, "what are you here for?"

I said to her "There's supposed to be a cyst." She told me to hold on, and that she had to get her supervisor. The supervisor came in and was the same technician that took the first sonogram. He said, "I don't know what to tell you, but we don't see the cyst anymore". He said, "There's not even like a trace." He said, "There's nothing there."

This is how God uses Pastor Bascom. She received her guidance, and she knew what to say. I listened to her, and followed instructions by faith.

I had one chart, the first one. And it showed this cyst. The doctors were worried. So they had brought me back a second time. And they were performing another sonogram to compare to the first one.

The technician was performing the second sonogram using the tool actually looking for the cyst, rubbing the "x-ray" on my belly. He was looking at the sonogram report that confirms there was a cyst there.

It had disappeared completely.

When I left with tears in my eyes I praised God and

thanked him for this miracle of healing my son. I told Pastor and she also praised God. She said to me, " God healed your son in your womb. He used the Communion which is the body and the blood of Jesus Christ.

It still brings tears of joy to me, what God did. I knew of someone who was pregnant and her child in the womb also had a situation. She had to go to a hospital where they had to do surgery on the baby while the baby was still in her womb.

So I truly thank God, and I am grateful to him and his servant Dr. Bascom because I did not have to go through that.

The miracles do not just happen ' on occasion.' Life brings unexpected situations, and when we least expect it, we are given a blessing.

My son was born Caleb. One day we were in church and was sitting in the back of the church this service. Pastor called me up. She asked me ,"If God told you to do something would you do it?" And I said " yes."

She told me that God said to change my son's name from Caleb to Immanuel (which was his middle name), that what we had was the right name but the wrong order.

She said, "God said to change his name from Caleb to Immanuel". She said, "Because God said that he's gonna change his name to change his destiny".

So we followed God's instructions. At this time our son was going on two so we had to legally change his name. The road has not been easy. Immanuel received early intervention and is currently receiving special education services. I don't receive any label or look at the circumstances because I know God changed his name to change his destiny and gave him His name, "Immanuel" which means "God is with us", so I know God is with him and us.

And I want to just to stay with Immanuel for one more miracle.

When I gave birth to him there were some complications during the labor. I started to get a fever, I had the shivers, and by that time, the doctors realized also that his heart rate had started to go up.

My OBGYN said, "You know what, we've been trying for the last couple of hours with your pregnancy, I think at this time we need to get him out and do a C-section. So they did the emergency C-section and Immanuel was placed in the NICU to rule out issues that may have been caused during the labor.

At this time I really was very strongly wishing for privacy, and I was given instructions by God regarding the company to keep around me at this delicate time. So to be honest I really wanted to be alone with God and my son. Since my son was in the NICU I had to walk over to that unit to see him because he had to stay in the "incubator". The NICU is the neonatal intensive care unit. So all the mothers were able to have their babies in their room for some time during the day but I did not.

I was very sad to not be able to see my son right away, to be able to hold him and spend time with him - my newborn baby!

But that time allowed me to read my Bible and be in constant prayer. I started getting visitors even though I requested to have none at the time. I became a little irritated and called Pastor Bascom. Truly I felt that after giving birth to my son, I had a way that I hoped there would be my way - my time with my son. Sometimes you value the company of others, and at times, you truly wish to have your time -- and for me - to bond with my son was the goal of my life right then.

Pastor always knows what to say. I always feel better after talking with her. This time though when I called Pastor she said too me, "I'm on my way." And I said to myself, on my way? She was going to come to the hospital? I had expected a phone conversation!

So thought "okay". And people give these testimonies of Pastor saying she's "on her way". So that was my first "on my way" experience and yes she was truly on her way to be used by God in such a special way.

Pastor arrived with two other sisters from the church. Pastor said to me, "where's the baby?" and I said, "he is in the NICU", she then says, "NICU?" I got up and proceeded down the hallway toward the NICU and in my head and I was thinking was that they don't let people in the NICU like that. I was asking myself, "What am I going to say?" I was asking myself how I could talk to the people there and would they allow me to see my son?

And here is where the miracle happened - because I buzzed the door, the doors opened,

and the nurse must've seen me.

She walked over, the doors opened. And to be honest, I don't remember introducing Pastor. But what I do remember is the nurse saying, "Oh come! I see the Pastor is here to pray for the baby". I was in total shock!!!!

The nurse took my son out of the little incubator. She gave Pastor a seat. She pulled the curtain and the nurse basically gave permission, in doing that. She gave Pastor Bascom the permission to "go ahead and pray for the baby".

This is a place where only the parents have an ID, which they check to make sure it matches the babies ID and check everything before anyone walks in!

God made a way for Pastor to come into the NICU, hold him in her hands and pray for him.

Tears just came to my eyes, 'cause God truly performs miracles all for his glory and uses my Pastor mightily.

Sixteen months later I had one daughter and there is another miracle concerning her.

My Pastor - she doesn't miss a step, Dr. Bascom.

Another miracle was with my daughter, she was born a healthy baby. I finally got to have her in my room after delivery.

Then, when Gabriella was probably a couple months along, she was very young, and I was doing her hair and looked as though she had a cradle cap. So I started treating her cradle cap with lotion and this rash started to come down to her face, her arm, her leg. And literally she was covered with this rash. I brought her to the doctor and he said it was eczema.

Having eczema as a child, I knew that it's itchy and at times irritating and painful. I was so very upset, and I was so worried - for my daughter had eczema all over her body. My poor little one was miserable. She was in such pain.

I told Pastor what happened and she prayed. There was one particular service when Pastor told Sister Edith to get her prayer shawl.

Pastor took her prayer shawl, and she wrapped my daughter in her prayer shawl and prayed over her. And I'm telling you, within a matter of days, it started flaking off. God performed another miracle and used my Pastor.

My daughter was healed from this skin disorder literally healed her from the crown of her to the soles of her feet. When I went back to the doctor he said said, "wow", "this is good", it's like she has newborn baby skin again" the ointment worked well.

It's funny - he thought I used ointment. But if he had asked, I know what I'd have said. It was a miracle from God. He used my Pastor and my daughter is healed.

I did not discuss it with the doctor.

But in my spirit I just said, "This is God's miracle right before your eyes."

"Right before your eyes this is God's miracle".

CHAPTER V

Ms. Maya Sheffield

MIRACLE

❖

"In everything set them an example by doing what is good. In your teaching show integrity, seriousness and soundness of speech…"
TITUS 2:7-8

After graduating high school I attended college and began to pursue a degree in nursing. Once I finished a couple of prerequisite courses, I then tested for the nursing exam. Weeks went by and I finally received my scores and I failed with very low scores. The thought of retesting was painful and discouraging. That night I prayed, and I asked God for guidance, and I asked him to reveal if this is the career I should continue to pursue.

One night during our church service, Pastor Bascom called me up, and God used her to tell me that I was in the wrong career. She told me to choose an occupation which I would enjoy working in. There were many options, but I buckled down, chose one and informed her that I wanted to be a teacher. With that she said, "Yes! God can definitely work with that."

Pastor Bascom prayed for me that night and with Gods instructions & directions I was well on my way to start my career and become a teacher. I researched and applied to many colleges that offered degrees in Education. In the Fall of 2013, I began my studies and after hard work, faith, and prayer I graduated Brooklyn College in 2017, with my Bachelors in Early Childhood Education and a Minor in Psychology.

God is so amazing, each miracle flows one after the other, they're all sequential.

Another miracle which God has performed in my life was when I was working towards becoming a licensed teacher . Each State has its Board of Education, and you have to pass the exams. In order to become a State-licensed Teacher, there are three exams that one needs to pass to be certified. Pastor Bascom would always pray for me and God would use her to encourage me that I would pass each exam I take.

During my undergraduate years in college I began to complete my exams so that I can be a teacher. The first test I took, I passed which filled me with excitement and much ambition. A couple of weeks later I applied to take another exam, once I received my scores, I became discouraged when

I saw that I failed. Many times, I rescheduled and retested but there was no change.

In the back of my mind I kept remembering Gods promise to me. This stage of my career was very trying. But I knew God had chosen this profession for me and giving up was not an option. I did some research and I came across a test prep course, which I eventually attended.

I then rescheduled the remainder of my exams, prayed many nights, studied, and used the skill and information I learned from the prep course and once I received my scores, I passed.

God gave me the courage and set me on my path to success! If at first you don't succeed, it is God's Love that will help you to try, and to try again!

Yes, Lord!! I passed all three of the exams!! I then received my license and I was qualified to teach. While this was happening Pastor Bascom had no clue that I was going through this metamorphosis. But God would always use her during service to let me know he hasn't forgotten about me, and that every test I take I will pass.

Why is it that God gives us Miracles? He brings forth His Miracles from Love and helps us to believe in Him. We are his children and he takes care of us.

One of His biggest all-time Miracles is helping us to have faith in ourselves.

The third miracle God has performed was blessing me

with a job in the Board of Education. The State Board of Education is known by everybody in teaching, whether it be the teachers, the Principals, the head of each School District. The Board of Ed. Is at the top and sets up the standards for schools. It is very important, and helps with codes of ethics, with laws and regulations – anybody working inside the Board of Education has had to pass very rigorous standards.

And that I would end up working at the Board of Ed. Is truly a Miracle!!

I would consider this to be a two-part blessing. In June of 2019, I left my previous job, I was working in a Pre-K center. It was the beginning of summer and I started to work at a summer camp. In my mind I was aware that school was going to start in September, and I needed to apply to jobs as soon as possible. After sending my resumé to many principals and expressing my interest in their school I received a call back from one of them.

The following week I went in for an interview and she informed me that if I am considered for the position, she would contact me by the end of the week. When I left the school, I prayed saying "God if this job is for me, I thank you for a response on Friday". My interview was on a Monday, and that Wednesday the principal called me. She told me that she was impressed with my credentials and she really wanted me to be a part of her team.

By this time, public schools were scheduled to open

within two weeks. I had been awaiting a response back from HR to finalize my employment. The HR department was on vacation and the principal was unsure of their return. One Wednesday night, we had a church service, and Pastor Bascom called me up. She ministered to me saying "you're waiting to hear some news regarding a job, and you are unsure what is happening, but God said not to worry, you will hear back from them soon." This night I knew God heard my prayers, Pastor Bascom was unaware of my situation, she didn't know I applied for a job and I was waiting for a final update. The very next day I received an emailed from HR stating my last steps to complete my employment. I was able to start in September as a Pre-K teacher working in the Board of Education.

This was September of 2019. I graduated college in 2017, and I completed my Board of Ed. tests in 2018. It can take time to go through the whole teaching licensing. So, in the summer of 2019, I became completely certified after passing all my exams.

So, I thought, "I'm thrilled to have this job!" and I started working in the Department of Education. It was amazing to have gotten all the way through my degree in Education, and my teaching license and then to have a job in my new career!!

Yet, God does not want you to just rest on your laurels, if He has more in store for you, He will let you know!! As it turned out, there was more in store!

In the process of taking my exams, Pastor Bascom had

encouraged me not to wait too long to go back to get my Master's degree.

She just felt this was a Word she wanted to pass along to me. God is so amazing, because she didn't know I had already applied for a Masters degree, after I completed my Bachelor's degree.

And with God's support, and the prayers of Pastor Bascom – I did go forward!

As I completed my Master`s degree God would use Pastor Bascom during our church services to remind me, that He has me covered and He will bring me through.

Recently, in the spring of 2020 I graduated with my Master`s Degree in Early Childhood Education!

So I have my Bachelors in Education, my State Board of Ed. Licensure, and my Masters in Early Childhood Education!

And I had thought that there was no end in sight when I left nursing, looking ahead at a big question mark. When I got held up with the licensing tests, I thought that was where my road to my new career was stopping. I thought I wouldn't make it to becoming a teacher. Yet, here I am – Bachelors, Board of Ed. License, and Masters.

God used Pastor Bascom to pray for me and keep me encouraged, knowing that with God all things are possible.

What better teaching in life, than the teachings of the Lord?

And Pastor Bascom is one of the teachers of the Lord,

she helps us to pray, trust God and be thankful for his miracles.

*"Although the Lord gives you the bread of adversity
and the water of affliction, your teachers will be hidden no more;
with your own eyes you will see them."*

ISAIAH 30-20

CHAPTER VI

Ms. Pia Ottley

MIRACLE

❖

My name is Pia Ottley, and I am a member of Dr. Bascom's church. I have been a parishoner at the Christian Crossroads Church since I was about 5 or 6 years old. I am now 38. That's a lifetime! It's remarkable, that I was truly "born" and I have lived my entire life, within the Pastor Bascom's Church!

I have seen the Church and Dr. Bascom herself, grow and develop through the years, and my heart and devotion to Christ have grown ever stronger through my relationship to the Christian Crossroads Church, and my experiences with our remarkable Pastor Bascom.

I am truly blessed beyond all I could have imagined in this life, by the miracles I have experienced, due to Dr. Bascom's extraordinary gifts and sharing with individuals who are in need of healing, of body, mind, or spirit. I am deeply blessed to have experienced the direct miracle of not just one, but two healing experiences with Dr. Bascom.

The first took place when I was 10 years old. Childhood is a time in which there is not usually caution about injury, and so children can at times be unaware of dangers. When I was 10 years old, I was in an accident that took place at home. This was very painful, and to a ten-year-old, very shocking and traumatizing .In fact, I had to have surgery for it. While usually a person may expect a surgery to go well, in fact, when the surgery was done, it caused nerve injury. You can imagine my own terrible upsetment, and that of my family, too. I did not know what to do, I was in pain, and I was afraid. At age ten, it was a terrifying experience to go through.

What happened to cause the accident? I was accidentally pushed onto a glass vase. The vase shattered and pieces of the glass entered my body in many places. It went in quite deeply, and was a danger, it could not remain in my body. So the glass had to be removed surgically. At first, I was in the Emergency Room. The doctors were able to take out some pieces in the ER. My painful ordeal did not end there, however. The doctors said they would have to take out the remaining pieces through putting me under anesthesia in the operating room. I had to have surgery. The glass had gone into my body so deeply that it had to be removed by a surgeon in the OR.

As a child, playing and running is part of everyday life -

it is without a thought that a child enjoys energy and fun! But in a moment this can change. What happened? It was very fast. I crashed into a big glass vase, in my grandmother's house. It shattered, and truly it was very frightening when I was cut, and the glass went deeply into my body.

We might usually have hope for medicine to heal us, and to help, and often it does. The ER doctors got out some of the glass. This was very helpful. But then they performed the surgery. It is hard to even say - they botched it and damaged my nerves. And the surgery left me walking with a limp. After the surgery, which was hopefully going to remove the deeply embedded glass, and help me to feel better, instead- I was left with a lot of pain.

I tried – it was something I tried to overcome. I tried to walk and hoped I'd be OK. But I experienced instead, that if I walked for any length of time, or if I ran, I had a bad pain in my ankle. The pain was chronic, and it was also in hip. And, it was in my back on my left side. My ankle was very weak and needed support.

This was after the doctors had done the surgery. They were done with what they could do. And I was left with pain.

We think everyday we can bear with pain, and overcome it, and bear the pain and go through it. But if you're trying to help other people, you need to have your strength to do that. And in my profession that is important -- because I'm a nurse. My goal is to help other people not to be the person who needs the help. So, on a typical day, I work 12 hour shifts, standing on my feet a lot, walking a lot. When my patients are in need of my physical help and support, I have to be able to turn them in bed, and to lift patients.

And so I would do it under duress in pain. I wanted to devote myself to my patients fully, and put all of my focus and attention on them, which is what they needed, and what I wanted to give!! But the pain I experienced was preventing me from giving my ' all,' and it made me very sad. I wanted to be my best for them. But I couldn't give as much as I wanted to, because I was held back by chronic pain from the old injury when I was ten years of age. It was years back, but that injury hobbled me every day.

I have for many years been active in the Church, which is an important part of my life. And, I am active in the community too, trying to bring awareness to important issues in people's lives, and help make everyday life better for everybody. One day in my community, we were having a domestic violence walk. This was a walk to offer support and fund-raise against domestic violence.

Pastor Bascom was there and she asked me, "How come you're not walking?" And I said, "Well, because of my ankle, I will be in pain if I walk for that long." Pastor Bascom said, "I didn't know that."

So from that day forward, she began to pray for me to have a pain free body. I had no idea anything might change in my life. I was so very surprised and it touched my heart deeply, that Pastor Bascom prayed for me. And lo and behold, after she prayed for me, it happened.

Now, I don't have that pain anymore. And I mean from that time forward, when Pastor Bascom prayed for me - I have been able to work my 12 hour shifts with no problem and no pains.

I'd had all this pain – I had walked with a limp. But it disappeared.

Not only did Pastor Bascom pray for me -- she also did a healing through touch. She put her hand on my left hip. That is the hip that I'd had chronic pain in for many years, since I was the age of ten.

And she prayed that I would have a pain free body, that I wouldn't have that pain anymore.

And after that – I'm telling you. I truly experienced a miracle. I had no more pain in my ankle, or my hip, or my back. It makes me still stop in wonder, and be so very grateful and thankful to Pastor Bascom and to our benevolent and healing Lord! I can smile about life now! I can even feel free to laugh, and to not worry about being in pain from my old injury. What is really remarkable? I will tell you: I can now work 12 hours, and you know, I'm standing up a lot, I'm walking back and forth, it's a very physically demanding job - and I don't have any more pain.

People may wonder - How did Pastor Bascom pray for me? Was it just once/ Or for an hour? Or more than once, and for a long time? Well, the miracle is even more profound. It was one time.

The day when she found out about my pain, Pastor Bascom said to me, " I'm going to pray for you in church on Sunday."

She prayed for me that Sunday.

And after that I had no pain anymore.

I had no pain yesterday. I have no pain today.

Looking back, before my healing with Dr. Bascom, I had to go back to the doctor a lot. And I had to do physical therapy. I was being told I had to have work, continually, to restore the working capacity of my nerves. But what happened? I was told that even if the physical therapists worked to get my nerves restored, realistically, this does not usually happen. Once nerves are damaged, they don't usually repair themselves. It was daunting - it was not easy, and there was not much hope that my nerves would heal. I thought I'd have the constant pain the rest of my life.

I went through a lot of physical therapy, acupuncture, chiropractors I went to see a lot of doctors, a lot of hospitals. But I nothing was of any avail. Nothing worked.

And then: Dr. Bascom prayed for me. It was one time, after she heard that I could not walk far, due to the pain.

And then: I was up and running again.

You might think that a miracle like this, which completely changed my life, happens only once. And it would truly be enough and more than I could ever have imagined. Pastor Bascom performed a healing with me, and I was healed.

So, to have a second healing -- it is hardly imaginable! But it happened to me, and it was again with Pastor Bascom.

I invested money with my relative. And it was over a significant number of years, the investment. It was an investment of money that took place over 15 years.

And I had got some of the money back like in installments, some of the investment. But it was not all of the money. It was just a portion, over time, and this was how the money was coming back to me - slowly, a little bit at a time. This was money owed to me - and it was not coming back to me easily. This was my experience with the payments.

But then for some reason God put it on Pastor Bascom's heart and she started praying that I would receive the balance of the money that was owed to me.

All of a sudden she just started praying, And she said to me, " I'm praying for you to get the rest of your money back."

I did not know there was importance to receiving the money back more quickly. I was not aware of what would happen, and what the future held.

But Pastor Bascom had a sense. And at the time she started praying. She didn't know it fully yet, and I didn't know it yet. But it was at a time that I was going to need the money. At that time I was in the process of purchasing a home and I was also in school to become a nurse practitioner.

I had not thought much about that money and anything other than the small payments. Because, I was working full time and making a decent amount of money.

But it turned out that I needed time off from work to complete my clinical work towards the degree. Because in addition to going to school full time, I had to complete a certain amount of clinical hours at the hospital.

It was too much at the time to work full time go to school full time and have a family and do clinical hours so I requested time off.

But as life would have it, at my job I was told, "We're too short staffed and we can't grant you any time off, we can't afford to right now." So then at work I was told, " If we don't give you the time off, are you prepared to resign?"

And I said, "Yes, I am." I don't know how I had the courage, but that is what I said. I felt I had to do it. School was more important. I was so close to being finished. Still, it was scary. Was it the right thing to do? How would I support myself and my family? How were we going to make it through, while I finished my degree?

I thought, " I'll speak to the Pastor about it."

Pastor Bascom felt the same way I did. She said ,"Oh, quit the job!"

But at the same time in my head, in the back of my mind, I was saying to myself, " Remember you have signed a contract to buy a house. And when you're in contract for a house, the banks want to see your steady income! What was I going to do about that? I didn't want to lose the house contract. I was so excited, with my family, to get this house.

Pastor Bascom at that time, said to me, " Oh, don't worry about it God will work it out." She had a faith so deep and abiding. I know my Pastor, I have known her for many years. I trust her. She had a sense of the future, and I could not see it, but she had the faith.

And so - in life, you can never know exactly what will happen, and how the miracle will manifest itself. Even if you can't see it in advance, then, there it is. It was truly amazing.

What happened? Well, a week before I was due to officially close on the house, who shows up? My relative I'd invested the money with. My relative came and brought a check, came over and knocked on the door. Now, I look back and I am laughing! It was more than coincidence! Much more!!

The money came came just in time I was able to quit my job, and finish school, and live off of that money, until it was time to get a new job and go back to work.

I got the house! I finished school, and I graduated!

Like I said, it was just so amazing that Pastor Bascom, she had a sense. And she had this faith. She started to pray.

Can you imagine? Bcause it was 15 years already that my relative owed me the money. But just for some reason Pastor Bascom just started praying for me to get that money and the money came right when it was supposed to.

In one person's life - just one individual - this might seem to be plenty, it would seem to be enough. More than enough! Pastor Bascom performed not just one miracle that deeply changed me life - she performed two. And you might think this is all and it is plenty!!

But that is not all - not all, by far. I have plenty more for you. We could be here til' tomorrow and I'd still be talking!!

Glory be to God, and to Pastor Bascom.

CHAPTER VII

Ms. Sherry Ann Joseph

MIRACLE

❀

My name is Sherry Ann, and I have had so many miracles with Rev. Bascom, it is hard to know even where to begin. I'm actually going to talk about four of the miracles. The first one occurred when I came to the Christian Crossroads (CCM) in July of 2004. I was invited by my coworker. At that time, I was attending another church, but every time I went to CCM on Wednesday & Friday evenings, I felt the move of God and decided to officially leave the other church and become a Christian Crossroad member in February of 2005.

I was born with a congenital heart defect called Wolff-Parkinson-White syndrome. It's basically a disorder where I could be doing nothing and my heart will just start racing and skipping beats. It was always frightening and just a horrible feeling! I didn't notice it until I was in my teens. I was sixteen or seventeen. What was it like? Well, I would have these episodes of rapid heart rate, dizziness, light headedness, chest pain, and difficulty breathing. At times it would be that I'd actually go through a bout of fainting.

Even though you might think people would say ,' Oh, that's a panic attack," - I was fortunate in that no one called it a panic attack. The doctors took it seriously, and when I was even younger - I was only 11 years old - I was diagnosed via a standard EKG. So, that's how I knew what it was. If I wasn't diagnosed, I probably would have thought I was having a panic attack. Because of the diagnosis at 11, my mom was very worried when I got these big symptoms in my late teens.

The doctors basically told her there was nothing they could do for me, but if I had some rapid heartbeats that she should just take me to the nearest emergency room and say "WPW." That meant she was telling the doctos and nurses,' my daughter has wolff-Parkinson-White syndrome, so they would know. But that didn't mean the doctors could do anything to 'cure' it, just knowing the name.

From my teens, onward, I was living life with a physical and an emotional imbalance, because I lived in fear. I didn't want to do too much. I never knew when the frightening and awful-feeling attacks would occur. My life was limited, hemmed physically and emotionally. When I was in my teens, I trained and I was a very fast track runner and I was forced to stop a few years later, with these severe symptoms. You can't have a crazily beating heart and sudden shortness of breath, and be a track runner.

Now -- my episodes in my teens weren't too frequent- maybe three. but when I got to my twenties, these scary episodes definitely increased.

To God be the glory, I'm alive.

I am alive!!!!

Yet there was a one sudden instance, I didn't know if I would be alive, and I'll tell you right here and now, this was God's miracle.

On Sunday morning, June 6th 2004, I was walking down an avenue, heading to my old church for service. And suddenly it happened - what I used to call the "episode." I basically started having an episode while I was walking. My heartbeat started going so fast, I could feel my heart pounding in my chest.

I was in a drug infested area known for having a lot of hookers, drug dealers, and drug addicts. It was not a good place to be by yourself while in a vulnerable state. I started having this pain and shortness of breath. Right then and there. I feared for my life, no one else was going to church with me.

When I felt it coming on, I said to myself, "oh no, not now." It was terribly frightening. My heart was beating out of my chest. I had a hard time taking a breath. Then I got lightheaded and I just blacked right out. Right on the street, with nobody to help me.

But then I knew. It was nobody else but God who was protecting me. I heard a very calm and quiet voice in my ear saying, "Get up, get up, don't worry just keep walking."

I then got up. And when I got up, I felt myself stumbling, but I was light on my feet. It was as though I was physically leaning on someone, but no one was there.

I saw people looking at me, so I figured they must have thought that I was strung out 'cause of course the area was known for that. I stumbled, but I didn't fall again.

I felt I was leaning on shoulders -- like the Lord was letting me lean on Him.

I finally made it to a big cross street. I stumbled across a wide avenue and I remember the light was green for the cars to go and I was still in the middle of the street.

There was an avenue bus driver, I could see he wanted to move ahead as he had the light. But instead, he held the traffic back and waited till I got safely across the street. I remember seeing him look at me and nod as if, to say, "You made it" At that moment, I felt this flood of relief, and I thought, "I'm safe now."

The church was literally one short block away. I went into the church. And when I got inside, the first thing I did was go to the bathroom. I started to wash my face. And everybody that knows me, knows that I'm very chipper, very upbeat. And at that time, one Sister noticed I wasn't.. She said, "What's wrong with you?" I said, "I'll be all right, I'll be all right, I'm just hot, I'm just tired." I didn't want to tell her right then, because- I just wanted the episode to stop. I was still having it, and it hadn't stopped.

I went into the sanctuary and started praying and crying. I was in so much pain. I was just saying, "Please, please, God, stop it, stop it, stop it!" But it wouldn't stop.

An episode would usually last for about three to four hours. I couldn't sit in church that long and be in pain, so I decided to tell one of the Associate Pastors. We then went into a private classroom with a couple of other people

They started praying for me and someone said ,"Call an ambulance."

I don't know what happened, but the ambulance was there within minutes. I think I fainted. When they got there, I was able to talk to them, and tell them what I had. The minute I said WPW, the EMT couldn't get my blood pressure. And I'm looking at him, into his face, and I hear myself asking, "What's wrong, what's wrong?"

Now a normal blood pressure is around 120/80. He could not get a reading on me. He could not find any blood pressure. The body has to have a blood pressure, it is the sign of life.

He finally got a reading after the third time, it was 40/20. And he kept asking me what my name was, where I lived and basic things that you're supposed to know. He was getting me upset because he kept asking me over and over. He would say so where do you live again? And I said, "I told you already."

I was getting mad at him, "I told you already! I told you my name, I told you where I live, what are you doing?"

He was just making sure I was coherent. So the EMT helped me at that point by saying, "Oh no, calm down, calm down, its ok. " And you know, I laugh about it now, but I realized looking back on the situation – what he was doing. He was trying to see if oxygen was getting to my brain. It is unusual for someone to have such a low blood pressure and be lucid.

Anyway, on my way to the ambulance, I had my tithes envelope in my hand. The "episode " was still going on, and I hardly had a pulse. But I stopped the EMT, and I said," I want to hand in this envelope!" I insisted!

Again he looked at me like I was nuts. I know he was thinking. "What is wrong with this lady? She is on her way to the hospital and is worried about giving in tithes."

I'll talk more about tithing a little later.

The EMT wheeled me into the ambulance. And when I got into the ambulance, they immediately started an IV. And I was off to the hospital. They rushed me to Maimonides hospital. We were there within six minutes.

When I got to the hospital, the medical staff was amazed. They were saying, "How is she talking and making sense?" Because, my blood pressure was so low, that I should have been unconscious, or delirious, but God definitely had his hand on me.

Then – when it's about 2 hours later, my heart rate is still ridiculously rapid at 376 beats per minute, but I was coherent with no organ failure. To give you an idea – do you know what the usual beats per minute are? A normal range would be in the 70s - 80s. If you run fast your beats per minute will go up to maybe low 100s. And I am at 376 beats per minute. What happens if it gets that high – is you can have a sudden heart attack or stroke. You are in an extreme danger range. That's where my heart was.

In order to get my heart back to normal rhythm, they wanted to use the defibrillator, the electrical pads that everyone sees on those hospital shows, but they didn't want to do it because I was coherent, and it would hurt. So it was a debate among the emergency staff as to if they should use the pads or not.

At this point I was so scared, I was crying. 'cause I see them in the corner, huddling, trying to figure out what to do. But I had an idea what was going on - because I'm a nurse.

I was in the ER, hooked up to the IV, my heart racing out of control, and I realized right then "Oh my God, this is gonna be the worst pain ever."

Because - well, they basically have to shock you, which means literally kill you – flat line you, and then shock you again to revive you.

All this is done so that the heart can return to normal rhythm. So in my mind I was right then thinking, "Oh my

God, I am going to see Jesus." Looking back, even if I'm laughing now - at the time I was so scared of the pain.

I was completely terrified. I was about be shocked with the goal to stop my heart.

You can imagine. My heart was going to be stopped. Then - hopefully - restarted.

The ER doctors gave me a sedative to calm me down because at this point I was saying to myself, "I don't wanna die."

Of course who wants to die? You know – you're thinking about it, physically and thinking "You're going to die."

Because - as a nurse, I already knew what the pads do and what they were for. I did not want to go through that.

Well - fortunately, the doctors ended up giving me another drug - and it worked. They never had to use the pads.

I said right there, "Hallelujah."

A normal pulse rate is from 80 to 100, as I said before, and my pulse rate was 376. So to get from 376 to even 200 was torture. I felt like somebody was pulling my heart out of my chest. It hurt so bad to slow my heart rate down. But the sedative definitely helped. And after they basically stabilized me.

The next day I was in surgery.

Prior to this day, I was going through these episodes with dizziness, light headedness, chest pain, throwing up, and a host of other symptoms. I was on different medications and the doctors said that they couldn't do anything for me. Around two weeks after the surgery, I was back at work because I was an agency nurse. I didn't get paid if I didn't work. I also had no health insurance. I had a diagnosed health condition, but didn't seek out a job with benefits. You know, as a young adult, you think, oh, I'm healthy, I don't need health insurance.

I know that from there on, my foot steps were ordered by the Lord.

Here is how the Lord guided met to meet Rev. Bascom.

As an emergency nurse, I was assigned to be an agency nurse at a community hospital, and so I went there and started working. I was definitely guided by the Lord. Because at that hospital, I met the coworker that invited me to Christian Crossroad Ministry, the Rev. Bascom's Church.

This coworker who welcomed me back to work, she was just always easy to converse with. I would talk to her often and confide in her.

I started telling her about a big financial stress I was having. I was just three weeks post- surgery, less than a month after I had thought my life was going to end. Three weeks later, I was getting non-stop phone calls from the financial investigator for repayment of the hospital bills that had accrued.

I tried to apply for Medicaid, but I was not approved. I had an enormous amount of bills. I'd had this operation that was required, and I didn't have health insurance. So you can imagine. I had hardly been healing from surgery and the investigator started calling about money. He was very threatening and would say, "If you don't work out a payment plan and start paying this soon, we're gonna garnish your wages."

My paychecks were going to be garnished, I could not afford the bills, I just had major heart surgery. I said this to the investigator, who was very hard-hearted in his response. He said, " Well think of this bill as having a brand new Mercedes in your chest." It was unbelievable. I was just in shock, how could he say that/ I had to have this operation and he made it sound like I just purchased a luxury car that was beyond my means! I felt like he was so insensitive and just started ignoring his calls.

To add insult to injury I would go to my coworker's office to vent. As a nurse, I was responsible for informing undocumented, pregnant women to sign up for free prenatal care and insurance for herself and her unborn child. The hospital gave undocumented women the opportunity to get free prenatal care. This was truly a blessing. And yet I as a U.S. citizen I was under tremendous financial burden and I could not get away from it. I was upset. Helping them truly weighed heavy on me each day, I was unable to pay the bills for the hospital surgery that had been necessary. That it was successful was truly amazing. But my life was under a very heavy stress at that time, the surgery was far beyond what I could afford. And the bills were due.

My coworker had advised me to talk to my old pastor

and let him know of the financial problems I was having. She said "as a tither, you can seek out help from the church and they should help." I followed her instructions, because I always tithed, even before going to the hospital. It was difficult to schedule a meeting with the pastor. Without getting much information or help, I figured I would just start paying the bill, little by little. But it was not going to be enough, and the pressure seemed like it would be never-ending.

Yet the Lord truly moves in mysterious ways. One day, my coworker was talking about the service she attended in her church and I just asked her where it was and if I could come.

Okay, here we come to the miracle of it all. I arrive at the Christian Crossroad ministry. Pastor Bascom did not know any of what that was going on with me. When the service was ending, she called me up to pray. She anointed me and prayed for me one time, and it wasn't even about my heart. The Rev Bascom just said, "Prince of Peace come on board and give her a state of peace. She said, "I see a lot of turmoil around her, and there's unrest, and she needs peace in her spirit, in her heart, and her soul."

And right then - what I experienced was - "Wow." I literally felt calmness.

Ever since I walked into the Rev. Bascom's Christian Crossroad ministry and experienced the "laying on of hands" I have never needed to take medication anymore. I have never had another "episode."

I forgot to mention that people have these surgeries and then - the surgeries do not necessarily work in fact, that can often be the situation.

So that's where the miracle comes in: mine worked! I never had to take medication, again, and I have never needed another surgery. I never had post-surgical complications and I never had to have constant visits to the doctor anymore about this.

I was healed!

And then to top it off, I ended up not having to pay the medical bills.

In another service, Rev. Bascom was led by the Lord, to pray for my finances.

In the end, it was all free; God took care of my debt. Through my faithfulness in tithing, He definitely poured out a great blessing upon me. So tie that all in and there's the great miracle. I basically walked into Christian Crossroads, sick and overwhelmed, but never had another issue concerning my heart. And then God sealed the whole deal by taking away all that financial stress.

That was one of the first times I walked into Christian Crossroads. And that's really what has kept me for multiple years. I've been there for 15 years now. And God let me know that's where He wanted me. He started me off on the right foot!

I have to reflect a little - I never fully understood the union between God and myself - and that I am a person to Him, and that I mattered. I was stressed, when God had already taken care of all the details.

When you go to a large church – that church that I used to go to was a 3,500 seater, you have a tendency to just go to church. It wasn't a personal relationship like it is now. Christian Crossroads is more intimate, it's more powerful — I knew this was where I belonged. That leads me into the second miracle because obviously staying in the church, I met my husband, or - should I say, he met me!

To make a long story short, we had two children after getting married.

This, unto itself, is my next miracle. Indeed, it is two miracles.

The next two miracles are in regards to both of my pregnancies. I must start by stating that I was born breech. My mom had me in Trinidad, West Indies. It was not common to deliver via C-section. If your baby's coming out feet first, then by God that's how the kid's coming out. So I basically came out into the world feet first.

I had two pregnancies. And I'm going to discuss the first one; a baby girl. The moment I found out I was pregnant, my husband and I were very happy. But then, when I was about 6 weeks pregnant, I thought I had lost the baby. At the time, I was working as a school nurse, I was doing my regular job, nothing strenuous, I was just standing there, and I had to go to the bathroom, and when I did, I said to myself after seeing blood, "I think I just lost the baby." I thought, "I'm having a miscarriage. It happens - and it is happening to me."

I pick up the phone, to call my husband. And when I spoke to him, I said, ' Honey, I think I'm losing the baby now. And he said, "Well what are we gonna do? " He was very quiet. I think we were both feeling, "There is nothing we can do." As a nurse, I knew if I went to the doctor, they were not going to do anything, it was a process that they were going to have to let happen. I knew the protocol for miscarriages. There is no intervention. You have to let it happen.

But when I hung up with my husband, guess what he did? He called Dr. Bascom. And when he spoke to her, she said, "Call your wife back and tell her get off that stupid job and go to the emergency room now!" My husband hung up the phone. Within 15 minutes he was at my job. With conviction, he forced me to leave the job. I then had to tell the Principal. I didn't want to tell her because I didn't want anyone knowing my business. But I had to tell her, there wasn't much choice.

The county hospital was literally five minutes away. When we got there, I let the staff know what was happening — I had on my uniform, so I guess they thought I was an employee. I got red carpet service — my nursing uniform was on! My Pastor had said, 'Go!" so I went, right away, from work.

I was examined and my blood was drawn quickly, but getting the results was at least a two hour wait. At that moment, everything just kind of came to a standstill. Nothing was going on and we had to go to church soon, so we signed out, and just went to church. I thought that was the end of it – that I had miscarried.

When we got to church, and told pastor what happened, she called me up to the front, prayed for me, and put her hand on my stomach. I don't recall every single word of the prayer, but I do remember her rebuking the spirit of death and calling for the blood to stop flowing. She had asked me if I had any previous abortions. I said, yes. After that, she called two other prayer warriors. She put her hands on top of my hands which were on my belly and rebuked the death angel. She then led me into a prayer of repentance. When I got home, I noticed the bleeding was very light.

Two days later, the bleeding had stopped, and I went to the obstetrician. She drew my blood again to see if my pregnancy hormone levels were going up. She told me to come back on Thursday to repeat the blood test & do a sonogram. When I went in, she put me on the sonogram machine and not even two seconds later, she saw the flickering of the baby's heart. She said "I don't know about you, or what happened, but there's a baby in there."

That's the beginning of the first pregnancy. My body was in crisis, and Dr. Bascom knew what I needed to do. She got me to the hospital. And then she prayed with all of her might and her connection with the Lord granted me immediate healing. God definitely used her to bring me through every step of the way.

Then, during the pregnancy, I had a horrible time with nausea and vomiting. I would constantly have cramping as well. The doctor had to put me on medication to stop the vomiting because I was losing too much weight. I didn't want anything except smoothies. At five months pregnant, I was already 2 cm dilated, the doctor had put me on bed rest. I was no longer able to work. In the early stage of pregnancy, if you dilate too much, you can lose the baby. .

So, now I'm on bed rest; I couldn't do anything, but I use to love to sing and dance and watch comedic shows. Around six or seven months, I went to the doctor for a trimester checkup and another sonogram. It was a Wednesday. After the sonogram, I got the news that my baby was breech.

I thought, "Lord, Jesus here we go again. " So now there's breech, where the feet, like I was born, were downward and the baby's head was upward. So while she was laying breech, all I did was pray, and sing.

During a church service on a Wednesday evening, Pastor Bascom prayed again, putting her hand on my stomach. She commanded the baby to turn and get ready for landing. On Friday, I asked the sono technician for another sonogram. She did it and couldn't believe what she saw. She was the same technician that did the sonogram two days before. She was excited and almost used up the sonogram photo paper because she took so many pictures for the doctor.

I just laid there and cried. God did it again! The sonogram revealed that the baby had turned and was in position.

Within 2 days, God used my Pastor's hands to prepare my baby for birth.

And that's truly a miracle. Dr. Bascom's prayers worked.

Most women have to go to a specialized hospital for breech pregnancies. I didn't have to do that. All I did was go to church, also known as the Christian Crossroad 'Hospital.'

About one month after that, I started having horrible dreams. One night, I dreamt that my front tooth fell out on the day of my baby shower. I immediately called Pastor because I knew that meant death. So we prayed again that the baby and I would survive the delivery.

On April 9th of 2011, I had a healthy baby girl. To God be the glory!

And now I have to give testimony about another of Pastor Bascom's healing prayers, and the miracle that took place, regarding my beautiful infant daughter.

When my daughter was nine months old, she was trying to walk, but she kept falling. When kids are learning to walk, they fall, they get up; I didn't think anything of it, but when she was 12 months old, she still had a hard time walking. She didn't walk till her 13th month. But what the issue was, prior to her trying to walk, I had not noticed. And it took my Pastor to notice- it was a problem with my daughter's feet. Her feet were basically turned outward; her toes were pointing outward to the side as opposed to frontward, this is also called 'Out-Toeing.'

I forgot to mention with my daughter, the reason she had a hard time walking and having issues falling was because in a baby the heaviest part of the body is the head. So when the child is breech, like she was, they're kind of laying on their legs and their legs are bowing while they're in the womb. So the weight of her head pushed down on her legs, and caused a curvature of her legs as well as "out-toeing."

When my daughter was 13 months old, Pastor Bascom was going to Panama again. She prayed for her. She laid her hands on my daughter's feet. She said, I want you walking by the time I come back. She was going to Panama for about 10 days. When she got back, we had church that Sunday morning, I'll never forget it, my daughter had a white dress on with green bows. My daughter loved to sit at the door and greet everyone who came in. When Pastor arrived and my daughter saw her, she jumped off the chair, and not walked, but ran to her without falling. And my daughter had not walked before.

That is the miracle. My Pastor's prayer worked. God healed my daughter!

After that miracle, Dr Bascom then gave instructions to follow through with. When my daughter was still less than 2 years old, my Pastor called me up and said, "You have to take her to the specialist to check her feet. They might have to break them or something, but take her to the doctor." This is a treatment if a child's legs are not growing properly, they may need to be ' reset' to grow correctly.

So of course I took her to the doctor. Pastor also said my daughter was going to need specialized shoes and therapy. When we get to the doctor, the doctor said "She doesn't need shoes or therapy, there's nothing wrong with her feet."

Her father's feet are like that, so I thought, ' OK, this is what the doctor says."

I then went back to Pastor Bascom and told her what the doctor said.

But that was not the end of it, because when the pastor tells us things, it's from the wisdom and the ushering of God. I knew I could not stop there. I took my daughter to the podiatrist on my job. He examined her and started her with leg braces, with a bar that connects both of the child's feet, and the bar is attached on the child's shoes.

After wearing the bar for only a couple of weeks, we were then able to get my daughter her specialized shoes. Pastor Bascom also continued to pray. Once again Pastor was going away to Panama. And she prayed for her and said to her, "I want your legs straightened."

Dr. Bascom called me up to the altar with my daughter. She put her in a chair. She got the oil, and she just rubbed her legs from knee to toe. Both legs. She kept going and kept going.

Then Pastor Bascom left for Panama. While she was away, I prayed at home too, and kept doing the oiling as well. And when she came back, my daughter's feet were straight.

And today my child's feet are completely straight! To God be the glory!

In order to keep the healing, we as her parents, had to pay extensive amount of money for orthopedic shoes. To this day I still buy custom orthopedic shoes for my daughter. Yet that is a part of the process for my daughter's healing and growth.

The miracle is that when the pastor prayed, we never had to take my daughter to the hospital, and she never had to have surgery.

And the bar that was put on her shoes? That bar didn't last for more than two weeks, we know for sure it wasn't the bar! It was God!

Nothing but the glory of God and the hands of Pastor Bascom, brought about this miracle.

And now we come to my second child – my son!

My son, too was breech, but for him he was a side-lying position, which caused him to be born with one foot turned outward and a shortened neck muscle; a condition called torticollis.

When he was about two months old, Pastor Bascom received this wisdom from God. She just looked at my son and said "Something is wrong with him."

She walked over to my son — all this time of course, my

son was going to the doctor for check-ups and he just got his shots. When the doctor saw him, these were regular visits there wasn't anything the doctor could see that was wrong.

But my Pastor looked at him for not even a couple of minutes during service, and said to me, "You have to take him to the doctor, something is wrong with him." God works in ways we may not fully understand, but we must follow. The Rev. Bascom couldn't put her finger on it, She just knew something was wrong.

I said to her, okay, I took him to the doctor again. And when I took him to the doctor, they said well we don't see anything wrong, and did a complete and thorough exam on him. So when they didn't see anything wrong, I came back to church and I told her.

And once again she stood strong in her convictions and said to me, "I don't care what the doctor said, take him to another doctor."

So basically, my Pastor kept saying something's wrong, something's wrong, and with our relationship, I knew she was right.

And soon after, one night I was praying for my son. Every night I pray for my kids. After I put him to sleep, I went to the computer to do some work. While on the computer, I heard a small voice whisper in my ear and tell me the name of my son's condition. The voice said the word : torticollis. Now I'm a nurse. I knew what it meant.(It's when the neck muscles contract causing the head to twist and be shorter on one side).

I then took my son back to the doctor. This time, when I took him to the doctor, I said,"My son has torticollis, please check him."

The doctor asked me to place him on the bed. And when I placed him on the bed, I took everything off of him. Upon examination, my son was not moving his left side. When most babies hear anything, they turn their head to the noise. And so if a baby is positioned straight they should be able to look to their left or right especially when music is playing. The doctor did that; he played music on his left side and tickled his left ear. And when my son didn't move, he said, yeah, he's not doing anything on the left side; he's got to get therapy.

He said, "Well, Mom - you're excellent."

And I said, "No, it's not me, it's God."

My son being a side-lying breech baby during pregnancy was born with a spastic neck

and again, as with my daughter before him, my Pastor prayed for my son to be turned in the womb. There are doctors that turn babies while they're in the womb. But I never had to go through that. They usually have to give you a sedative and turn the baby. I never had to go through any of that. It sounds magical, like oh, okay, the baby's turned. Of course there were things going on in my stomach. But the feelings in my stomach were light enough where it didn't disturb me, and once again God did it.

Once again I took a sonogram and it was confirmed, my son was in position for birth!

God's wisdom guided Pastor Bascom through the pregnancy and birth of both children. All the way through, my Pastor conversed with the Lord on my behalf, took guidance from Him, and offered prayer.. She could 'see into' the situation and knew what was needed to bring in the healing of God.

For the torticollis, my son had to go through a series of physical therapies, the first three years of his life. The muscles on his left side were not fully formed, so the physical therapist would come to the house, and exercise my son's neck, and force him to use his left hand, she even prayed! When he crawled, his left wrist was weaker than his right, it would buckle under him as the muscle was not fully developed. It was the Rev. Bascom who said my son needed to be looked at, and prayed so that I did not complacently take ' no' from the doctor.

And so, here we have my two children, whose lives came into being with problems that could have been much worse, and were spared much physical pain , and miraculously they were healed.

My family was in the care of God, we received miracle upon miracle. I didn't have to go through strenuous procedures for during the pregnancies, for the birth of either of my kids. This was just all done through prayer and the hand of God-truly miraculous.

Well, here I come to another miracle I will talk about

now, but I am sure there will be others.

So basically this miracle is about the Lord guiding me to work at the current hospital I'm in.

I was going in the vicinity of the hospital. I would go regularly for appointments with my son. And when I'd pass by the hospital, I just felt like offering a prayer, "God, I would love to come back to work here 'cause it would be so close to home, and I'd be able to be with the kids more."

I didn't say anything to anyone. It was just a thought that took place when I was passing the building. And I think that night we had church. And I went to church.

During church service, Pastor called me up. And she said, "You know, I don't know why, but I feel the need to pray for you to go back to this particular hospital."

And she prayed.

Lo and behold – wow. Not even a week later, I got a phone call from my old supervisor. She just called me out of the blue and said, " You know, I was just thinking about you, would you like to come back here to work? " And I said, "Yes, of course."

She then put the paperwork in for me. she said, "Well, the good thing about it is I'm glad you wanna come back, but I only have two positions. One is per diem and one is part time." So I said, "Well I do want it, but I don't know which one I wanna take yet, let me call you back."

So, of course I called Pastor Bascom and she was in awe.

She couldn't believe that I got the phone call so fast. So I told Pastor the offer, and she said, "Just take the part time and get in the door. We don't care as long as you get in!"

I called my supervisor back and told her that I would like the part time position. She's said, "Really" She had thought the part-time might not be enough, and that it would disappoint me. But I said, " Yes, it's fine, I'm fine with that." My boss was so happy to have me return!

I was basically part time for about five years. And while I was there, I didn't fuss, I loved it. And I ran into Pastor Bascom in the hospital a few times.

And she said, " Wow, you're so happy!" I responded, "I love it here!" And Pastor Bascom said, "You know, God really did it for you."

During this time, Pastor and I never discussed that I was at that point just part-time.

Now looking back, I needed to be part time because I had a lot of appointments and the kids had too many days off from school.

In 2017, I remember Pastor asking me what was going on on the job? I said, "I'm still part time and it's fine, it's great, I need the time because the kids have too many holidays in school." My husband being a full timer, he couldn't take off as easily as I could. So I was part time. I was only working three to four days a week. For me, it was easy to juggle around the holidays and things like that. I was never stressed by work— but if I had to come to work five days a week, I couldn't have done it. At times, we had the help of my husband's grandmother and some of my church sisters as well.

In April of 2019, I didn't tell Pastor anything about still being part time, but one day she just called me up to pray. And she said, "I don't know why, but are you working part-time?" And I said, "Yeah."

The Pastor said, "You need a full time job."

And in my mind, I didn't know if I could do full time with the kids.

But the Rev. Bascom, prayed for me on a Wednesday. And on Thursday, one day later, I looked at the job board at work, and I saw there was a full-time position open in the Emergency Department. I went to the Nurse Recruiter and asked if I could have it. She said, "If you want to work in the Emergency Room, it's yours."

What a miracle! My Pastor, Rev. Bascom, prayed on a Wednesday and on a Thursday, I had a full-time job in my workplace!

You would think ' Wow, that has to be the end of all the miracles!"

But, it is important to say how everything worked out.

Just when you think life is settling down – we had to move.

After moving on the border of Brooklyn and Queens, in NY, I thought, oh my God, our new apartment is going to be just too far away from work, how will I ever get there and back?

But to God be the glory, I discovered there is a bus stop, right near our new home. And when I got to the bus stop and saw the destination sign, I found out - the bus goes all the way to the hospital where I work! To this day every time the bus pulls up and I read the destination, I praise God!

I never thought in a million years the bus would be a direct route right to work. I do not have to travel on a train, or do a transfer. Even when the weather is bad, I literally walk one block to the bus, and when I get off the bus, I walk right into the door of the hospital.

The Lord - he just put it all together. And he took care of all the details.

So that's about it - a few great miracles! And each one, from the heart and hands of the Rev. Bascom, to God, and then from the Lord, over to me. God is good and I am grateful.

The Lord works even from generation to generation.

From a mother to her children, and from her children, to the world, and back again.

He bestows His miracles on us.

CHAPTER VIII

Ms. Theresa Faison

MIRACLE

--- ❄ ---

I've been at Christian Crossroads all my life! I want to tell you about the amazing Miracle that was bestowed upon me by Pastor Bascom.

Let me sum up what happened, first and say: "Wow!!"

In my story of this Miracle - you will see what I mean!

There are many Miracles at Christian Crossroads! The main one I'll talk about is - the time that Pastor Bascom threw a lifeline out to me in her prayers, and the Lord was attached to that lifeline! I was buoyed up and I was able to fulfill a dream of my lifetime.

My dream was to be able to go back to school.

I didn't just do 'ok,' as it turns out I really got to the place where I am now able to do my true work in life.

And Pastor Bascom - she has been at the center of it all.

What happened was pretty amazing. You have to know a little more about me to know why.

Okay.

The first miracle is I was able to take blood.

And right here I know that stops you in your tracks – I mean, what is that – taking blood? I did what?

I am a health provider. That is what Pastor Bascom's prayers helped me to become. It is my dream work.

But here is the glitch: If you don't know the first thing about taking blood, you will never make it.

Why? Because my specific role is that I am a Phlebotomist! So our stock in trade, what we do all day long and what is supposed to be a very special skill for a Phlebotomist, is we know how to take blood. We are the specialists in that, in the hospital, the nursing home, what have you. We are the profession that knows how to do this. We are called in for that and everybody else – the doctors, the nurses, everybody – turns to us to take the blood!

So what do I need to know how to do really well?

Take blood!

But it is not that easy at all! It is not just the physical, it is never just routine mechanics. You do not just poke somebody's arm and draw blood. You ever try to find that vein in a person's arm with a lot of flesh, or a person who is dehydrated? Or a person who is very tense and keeps pulling away? You have to know what you are doing.

You also have to have the right touch. Getting that right touch is everything.

I'll say what I mean, imagine you have a patient who is 80 or 85 years old and you have to draw blood. You are holding this very frail arm of a person with paper-thin skin. You know it is not what they want to have done! It is going to cause a moment's pinch but for that elderly patient, there maybe a lot of fear. And maybe the person doesn't know just what is going on. The mind might not be all there, in some. You want this to be fast, accurate, no fuss. So you hold that frail arm, and you have to find the place to draw the blood and it is not always easy. You have to look, be focused, and be caring, and you need the right touch.

OK, here again imagine a little baby. It is not uncommon you will have to draw blood from a neonatal baby, or a baby with a heart problem, or a baby who is sick and crying. The last thing you can do is explain to that baby who doesn't know who you are and is maybe in pain - you cannot have a conversation. You have to be very careful, and you have to concentrate, but there are distractions - flying feet, crying. A lot can happen without notice. You have to keep that baby safe, and draw blood - fast, accurate, and with the right touch.

I went to school, and I was so happy to do my training!

But when I went through the classes to learn to take blood as a Phlebotomist, they don't really teach you how to really take blood on babies and the elderly or those who have small veins, or a whole host of situations you run into every day.

Did you know you may need a bigger needle, or a very small one? There are teeny tiny needles, you have to know how to work with those. And it is not just the arm - in a tough situation it might be the top of the hand, the side of the wrist, even between the toes.

I was having difficulty and apprehensive taking the blood especially from newborns and the elderly. And I didn't say anything to anybody. Yet there I was and I really was not sure I could do it. It was not something you can suddenly figure out - things that come up can be a problem - there's a lot. You know you have to be very careful and also you need confidence too, because it is what you have to do.

I was a Phlebotomist by training but in the actual moment, you have so much to think about, and I had my doubts.

Then - something really truly remarkable happened.

God used Pastor to tell me that even though I was having issues and doubts, and that I would end up being one of the best at taking blood.

And the next time after she prayed, I am right in the middle of being with a patient. I was preparing the arm.

You know you use the tourniquet, and you have to look and see where to draw the blood. And there is no map in front of you.

I am there with my patient.

And I saw a light.

OK that is about as odd as saying it.

You can hardly imagine. I knew this was not a figment of my imagination. Right on this patient's arm - I saw a light. And that light lit up, and it showed me exactly where to go to take the patient's blood. And when I tell you, I went straight in, I got the blood - you can imagine how I felt. I just followed that light and there I was, in the right spot.

And this was an older difficult patient - we deal with the hard patients for drawing blood daily. And I'm usually unable to draw her, but this day I was able to draw blood with no problems.

Pastor prayed for me. I was not thinking about the prayers. All of a sudden, this light was shining, right where I needed to draw the blood. No ray from the window. No flashlight. Nothing.

There was this light it was a guide.

And I realized, "I am being guided by the Lord and Pastor Bascom."

That line of light - that was Pastor - and God - a team.

And from that day, I am one of the best at my job. If

there's any issues, they come to me and they ask me to draw this baby or to draw this older person. Whoever they can't find the vein for, I'm able to get the vein 100 percent.

Pastor had a line of light to the Lord.

And God heard her prayers.

He placed His Light right in front of me.

That was Miracle #1.

Ok. Here is this next one.

I was going back to school for training to be a Hemodialysis technician. That is a different training from Phlebotomist. You know with the blood again, but dialysis, like what kidney patients have to do. It is very specialized.

I wanted to go back to school. But I was having issues with my job because my supervisor at the time, she wouldn't allow me to take the time to switch my schedule to do so.

And do you know how Pastor Bascom is?

She'll get to praying!.

And she prayed that the supervisor would be removed from that position. And she was removed from that position. I was able to speak directly to my manager. My manager worked it out that I was able to switch schedules. And I was able to go back to school.

But on top of that, just looking for the schoolI could go to - which was itself was very difficult. And pricing for the schooling was either $6,000 to $8,000.

And I'm thinking, " That's a lot of money, that is just

too much."

I don't know how this is going to work out. But with continual prayer, my Pastor got to the right place. We found the school, and the pricing was only $2,200 for the entire course. And I mean when I tell you, it was just right, the location was only 30 minutes from home, and it fit the schedule for me because it was only on Saturdays that I had to go.

There I am - in school for the Hemodialysis Technician training!! I felt so blessed!!

But I was having difficulty picking up the material, you know, the school and training - it is a lot to study and do.

And again without saying anything, God used Pastor to say I was having issues understanding what the professor was reviewing.

Pastor prayed that I would have retaining power and a photographic memory.

God showed me how I need to study. I went from being afraid I would fail, to the next time I took my exam, I received a 90. Then I finished the classes, and I finished as one of the top.

So you know, I am eternally grateful for my Pastor Bascom for praying, because now I have another career goal that I can move into. And the fact that I was able to get that schooling for that price is a Miracle and a blessing in itself.

Because like I said, every other school was either $6,000 or $8,000. So to be able to get that course for only $2,200, that is a big difference. I was able to pay the bill off and continue with my career.

When Pastor finds a line in with the Lord, your life opens up in a new direction, and there is a light shining upon you.

What Pastor and God did was a Miracle - more than one!

They placed the Light right there in front of my eyes.

CHAPTER IX

Ms. Shana Thomas

MIRACLE

❋

My name is Shana, and I am a long-time congregant in Pastor Bascom's Church. I have been a religious person for my entire life. I have always believed in our Lord on High and in the teachings of the Bible. In my prayers, I seek guidance daily from the Lord and his word. I read the lives of the Saints. I have always felt that humanity, if we followed the teachings of the Bible, we should seek every day to 'do good' in the world. So I have had a faith in my fellow man. I had a sense of God as all powerful. And people could do good. And in between — the Saints truly brought the Word of God to humanity. My goal in life was to do good work, and follow the Lord.

Yet never did I think that the Hand of God would reach out to me through his faithful Servant, Pastor Bascom. The Miracle that came upon me, opened my heart and my body -

to the Lord's Healing powers.

I have come to see the power of Dr. Bascom's extraordinary faith, that God would chose to bring His Healing to me, through Dr. Bascom.

One Friday afternoon, a day that was normal for me, became one that was unlike any other in my life. I usually find myself in good health. Yet that day changed my view of the world, and I came to understand that a sudden shock of pain, could come upon a person. And just as powerfully, even more so - that pain could be made to disappear.

One Friday afternoon, I was experiencing very sharp stomach pains, so my mother rushed me to the emergency room for them to check me out. When we arrived, the doctors asked me a lot of questions about the symptoms I was experiencing. Afterwards, he scheduled me to take a variety of test to find the reason for my stomach pains.

When the results came back the doctor discovered I had a 7 cm ruptured cyst on one of my ovaries and the other one had a 4 cm cyst. I was admitted into the hospital that night because they said I needed surgery right away. My surgery was scheduled for Sunday afternoon.

I remember the morning of my surgery my mother and my pastor were on the phone praying for me and my pastor sent the word that my surgery would be a success. I was discharged from the hospital on Monday and I went home in a lot of pain.

On Friday, I went to church and my pastor called me up for prayer and the lord touched my body. He healed me. I walked into church with a lot of pain and walked out with no pain. I had an appointment scheduled the following week and when he examined me, he saw that the 4 cm cyst was no longer there.

When he did the sonogram, he did not see it on my ovary anymore.

The Doctor was surprised and said "Oh My God!" He did not see anything. It was no longer there. I was shocked myself. Because I was expecting him to say something about the cyst. I no longer had doubt and I knew it was nothing but God. So, I said, "Thank You Jesus" and he said "yes, thank you Jesus."

When I left the hospital, with my discharge papers and my medicines, I was not able to walk easily. I was still in pain. I was told by the hospital that it would take time and that slowly I would feel better. That was somewhat reassuring, but I wondered how long it might take.

The surgery saved me from a lot of very significant danger, and maybe even helped save my life. But it didn't make the pain go away, after surgery it was not suddenly 'great.' I did not know what to expect.

Was I going to be in pain for a long time? Would this stomach pain be in my body for days? Or weeks, or months? The pain wasn't just disappearing, and it was hard to face. I didn't know when or even if I would feel really - better. I knew the doctors did not know for sure, either. This was going to be a 'wait and see' situation.

I was discharged from the hospital on Monday and I went home in a lot of pain. I was at home for 3 days, and each day it was hard. I was struggling to sleep, to sit, to walk. I was waiting and I was afraid as each day, I still had this pain. It was after the surgery, and it was definitely a situation that was ' better' than before the surgery. But pain is not something you can ignore. I didn't know what would happen. I just knew it was still there, and not 'a little better ' every day.

For three days, then — I was at home, after the surgery . I had surgery Sunday. I went home Monday. Tuesday, Wednesday, Thursday, the daily question I asked myself was: When will this go pain away? And the harder question: Is this pain here to stay?

On Friday, I went to Church. It was tough to get there, but I knew I had to go — I wanted to be with my Church, and my Pastor. It was very important for me to be there, and to pray. When I arrived, just sitting in the sanctuary made me feel safer. But I was in pain when I arrived, and as I prayed, I tried to put the pain out of my mind.

Then, and my Pastor called me up for prayer.

When Pastor Bascom called me up for prayer, the Lord touched my body.

He healed me.

I walked into Church with a lot of pain and walked out with no pain.

Praise Be To God! I know, without any doubt, that a miracle was visited upon me by Pastor Bascom. The Hand of the Lord came through Pastor Bascom, and when she prayed with me, and put her hands upon me, the Lord worked a miracle upon my being.

I walked out the door of the Church, at the end of prayer — pain free.

Well, in life experience — that's a major development.

I always ask whenever I see people with miracles, I'm always interested in people who have some information like radiology charts. They have clear records, direct evidence. And then — when I talk with people who have had a Miracle of Healing - that medical evidence — after the Miracle — it has changed.

And this is what happened to me. There was a cyst, that was physically identified, and now it is no longer there. The doctors can't explain that unless it was misdiagnosed. But this was not just one person — tests are looked at by more than one doctor, by several experts. The tests require skills, and training. Then the results are looked at by more than one doctor. The doctors look at each others results.

These are independent reports. So — were there that many mistakes in a row? I think it is unlikely — I don't know about that! Medicine might no be able to explain everything that takes place in the body! But doctors have developed good tests to ' see what is going on.' And a big cyst is a flag waving up and down. It requires medical intervention.

What happened to me was that there was a cyst, and then - it disappeared. I had a huge amount of pain before the surgery, and then pain afterwards.

This was my Major Miracle.

I was healed by Dr Bascom directly from the Hand of God.

It can take a Major Miracle to wake you up to the powers of the Lord.

Looking back, I realize that there were other Miracles in my life.

When I attended high school, one of my teachers said that my class was not college material. However, he was proven wrong because with the prayers of my pastor who always prayed for me and advised my mother to get her dress ready because she was going to graduation.

I went on to Brooklyn College and graduated with my Bachelor of Arts in Early Childhood Education.

I am now working as a Teacher and studying to receive my certification license to work in the Department of Education. Furthermore, with the continued prayers of my Pastor and my mother I will finish my Master of Science also from Brooklyn College in Speech Language Pathology and I cover this under the blood of Jesus Christ. We must always remember what the Lord has done for us. To God be the Glory for all he has done!

I went to Church, and I experienced there the prayers of my Pastor. My Pastor always prayed for me. And at the time that I was being told by my teacher that I likely was not going to college — my Pastor went to my mother. She advised my mother to get her dress ready because she was going to a graduation.

And Lord be Praised — my Pastor was right.

We must always remember what the Lord has done for us. To God be the Glory for all He has done!

CHAPTER X

Ms. Venancia Thompson

MIRACLE

---   ❀   ---

Then shall thy light break forth as the morning,
and thine health shall spring forth speedily and thy righteousness
shall go before thee; the glory of the Lord shall be thy reward.

ISAIAH 58:8 (KJV)

In the Bible we read, of God's great healing powers. Psalms 107:20 says that God sent His Word and healed us and rescued us from the grave.

I love my church and my Pastor. God has used and is still using my Pastor in a mighty way in my life and my children's life. God has endowed her with godly divine knowledge, wisdom and above all understanding to guide each one of us through difficult situations that we may face throughout our journey of life. Prayer brings the answer to every situation in our lives. When things seem hopeless and even sometimes impossible, God says, don't look at the bigness of your problems but at the bigness of your God. He specializes in making things that seems impossible; possible. As Luke 1:37 says: "For with God nothing shall be impossible".

I cannot tell my story or the miracles that God has performed in my life and my daughter's lives without acknowledging and thanking God for my Pastor, the scalpel that He has used mightily. Her commitment, availability and the exemplary life that she has lived as a battle axe for God, has made her a vessel that God has used to fight battles for us. Her sensitivity to the Holy Spirit guides her when it is time to pray and how to turn to our Lord for the answer.

Our tribulations first started with my youngest daughter, Sumayyah Roberts. In late 2012 early 2013, she was losing a lot of weight and was always tired. I took her to her doctor and they ran some blood tests and then just sent her home.

But when we went to church, I told Pastor that she was losing a lot of weight and Pastor prayed for her. This was on a Sunday. Two days later, Tuesday night while at home my daughter felt extremely tired. She was lying on the coach she stood up and said, "Mommy I cannot breathe." And she was holding her chest. I proceeded to call 911 and I called Pastor Bascom. Pastor picked up the phone on the first ring, and she prayed. She told me to right away call 911 and take my daughter to the emergency room.

That night Pastor was in the middle of service at her home and she said while praying that God put in her spirit to rebuked the Death Angel. She sensed the death angel was lurking around, even before I called her. Normally when she is having service she does not pick up the phone for anyone. However, that night Pastor said that the Holy Spirit told her to pick up the phone. Thanks be to God on High that my Pastor was in tune and obedient to God's Spirit to pray and rebuked the death angel from advancing.

The ambulance came and they rushed my daughter to the emergency room. When we got to the emergency room she was unconscious. The doctors immediately intubated her and ran extensive blood tests. At this point they still didn't know what was going on in her body and had not yet narrowed it down to what it was. After waiting for about one hour for the blood test results, my daughter's blood sugar count went up far beyond normal. When we first got to the Emergency Room her blood sugar was 500. The doctors still running some other tests her blood sugar count went up dangerously to 1,400. The doctor stated to me that a child or adult with a regular blood sugar count will be from 70 to 100 in children, and a little higher in adults; having it as high as 500 was way beyond normal and dangerous but 1,400 was extremely dangerous and fatal.

In fact, the doctors and nurses that night told me that if we hadn't brought her in to the Emergency Room that night, she would have gone into a coma and died. I Thank God for my Pastor who prayed and stood in the gap for my daughter that my daughter is still on this side the land of the living.

The tests results came back and she diagnosed with Type 1 Diabetes. My daughter was immediately admitted and remained in the hospital for approximately two weeks under medication and a strict diet in order to normalize her blood sugar count.

I cannot thank God enough for using my Pastor so mightily and all her prayers. The Lord is going to richly bless her for her labor of love.

God used her to save my daughter's life and I have no doubt that He already saved her soul.

My daughter was 15 years old when all of this happened. She is now 22 and thanks be to God, she is in good health. I have no doubt that God healed her.

The miracles didn't stopped. We served a mighty good God who love us so much that He sent is only begotten Son that whosoever believe in Him will not perish but have everlasting life.

Fast forward between 2013 and 2014, I had my monthly and was abnormally bleeding heavily and profusely to the point that I was feeling weak and tired for a couple of weeks or more. I went to church on a Sunday still bleeding profusely and feeling weak and dizzy I couldn't stand up and not alone get out of my seat. My daughter told Pastor and she called me and prayed for me. After she prayed, the blood flow slowed down that I was able to drive home. She gave me instructions to make some home remedies to take. I took the home remedies and felt better however in the middle of the night early morning I started bleeding again profusely while I was in bed. I got up and went to the bathroom sat on the commode and all the blood that was left in my body came gushing out. I closed my eyes and bowed my head; everything went black and I collapsed on the bathroom floor. I was cold and I felt my Soul leaving my body. And I saw my Soul traveling through a tunnel.

Thank God my youngest daughter was at home with me. She heard the noise of me collapsing on the bathroom floor; she opened the door and screamed, "Mommy, Mommy get up, get up, don't leave, don't leave me!!" I heard her screams and her cries, I said within myself I cannot go out like this Lord. After that I felt my Soul coming back into my body. I got the strength to sit up and I open my eyes and told my daughter to call 911 and call Pastor.

The ambulance came and rushed me to the emergency room. Still bleeding profusely, they ran some test and checked my blood; my hemoglobin was down to 6. By the time I was admitted my hemoglobin was down to 5. A healthy person's blood count is double digit (12 to 16). This was dangerously low.

I thank the Lord that my daughter was at home that day

because both my daughters would have come home and found me dead in a pool of blood.

I thank God for my Pastor praying and sending the word when my daughter called her. God saved my life and He saved my soul. Why? Because God has a plan and a purpose for my life that I must fulfill, so I can't leave yet.

After being admitted in the hospital for about three to four days; the doctor's said to me you lost so much blood, we don't understand how you're still alive. You should have been dead. I had to be given a blood transfusion because of all the blood I had lost. They couldn't understand how I was still alive.

It was by the grace and mercy of God that I am here. And thank God for my Pastor, her life is completely devoted to God and that is why He can use her in our lives. The Holy Spirit makes her so sensitive when something is going on with us; she is able to know, pray for and turn it around.

I thank God every day for my Pastor being in my life, and my daughter's life. He worked in her and through her to bring about the miracles in our lives.

And my own health is good, too, along with my daughters.

This was an experience like no other; words will not be enough to explain the battle within me; because you're living it. You hear and see these things on TV, but this was real. This was so real. God is real!!!

He's not through yet with me.

My life and my daughter's life are no longer ours, it belongs to God. Thank you Jesus!!

God out did Himself once again. I was experiencing upper and lower back pain, neck pain which also caused me to have bad headaches. I went to the back/spinal specialty clinic and they did several MRI's and I was diagnosed with bulging herniated discs throughout my spine, from my neck all the way to my lower back. Several discs were bulging and herniated. The doctor said that in order to correct this problem they will have to do surgery. This extensive surgery was not covered by my insurance so in order to get the surgery done I would have had to pay a co-pay of $7,000. After the surgery I would have had to go for weekly therapy which would have required additional bi-weekly payments every time I went.

I went to church and I told my Pastor that I was having upper and lower back pain which was giving me headaches and I went to the doctor and they told me that I needed surgery and that my co-pay for the surgery was going to be $7,000. She told me that she experienced something like that and that she had that same surgery and it didn't help nor it will work.

So she said, "I am going to God. Under the anointing my Pastor prayed for me and I went down to the floor and while I was down on the floor I felt a heat going up and down my spine.

When I got up, the pain was no longer there.

The following church night I told her that when I was on the floor I felt a heat going through my body, up and down my spine, from my neck to the lower part of my back.

Pastor said, "Oh, wow that was the Holy Ghost, He was healing you, He healed you."

I didn't need the surgery. I didn't need to pay $7,000 for co-pay. God used His servant and He healed me.

Look at God, He is an awesome God.

I thank God for Jesus and how He uses my Pastor in every area of our lives; where He uses His wonder working powers to perform extraordinary miracles.

God is constantly performing miracles for His people and He wants us to share our testimonies to the world to let them know that God is real. If He did these things for me and my daughter He can do it for them. He is a Healer, a Deliverer and that there is nothing impossible with God if you believe. Amen!

CHAPTER XI

Mr. Valentino Vaughn

MIRACLE

--- ❈ ---

The world is a large place in which we live our lives, each day not knowing what will happen! Will the day go as planned? And will our station in life be one that improves, turns downward, or stays the same? We do not know what is in the Lord's plan. It can be a beautiful journey each day! And there are many times, looking at the road ahead, you can see,' I have a good life! One's prayers are answered when each day life is filled with the gratitude of dreams fulfilled.

Yet how many times is it the case that there are bumps in the road? Many days the bumps can be felt, small or large. You suddenly come upon a time when you realize,' Just ahead of me there is a rough patch!" And you ask yourself, "How will this turn out?" It can be frightening, as we do not know the future. We see that tough time ahead, but not how it will turn out.

The trouble can be small -- or it can completely upend your life. The solutions may be within your personal reach. Or - when you come up against a situation that is bigger than you are, you may feel helpless. What can I do? For we are individual people, with limits to our powers.

We are not alone. This lesson I learned through the times when trouble hit. it can take a bigger, Higher Power, to step in. And then you know, without a doubt, you have received a miracle.

My story is just that. I hit a very rough patch, and there was no way around it. I had to find a solution, but my powers were limited. ' God, please help me in my hour of need.' You may pray to the Lord on High this way. But what if you are not the one who can do this for yourself? You may need the help of those who have such a close relationship with God, that they have a direct line in — the urgent call is heard! And I am here to give testimony. The Lord in his great powers, He knows. He hears. He responds. How do you know? The signs are as clear as day!

Here is my rough patch in the road. What took place was that I landed in trouble, and I did not have the power to find a solution. Yet we know who did! Our Lord Almighty.

During my enlistment in the US Marine Corps, I was stationed in Paris Island, South Carolina. We had a big Marine outfit there. And it turned out, that we were informed that 120 Marines were being investigated by the Immigration and

Naturalization Service for not having valid Visa or Green Card. I know you'll wonder — can a U.S Marine be under this type of inquiry? A Marine is serving the country, you train hard, and you devote yourself to protecting the citizens of the USA. We are groomed to respond to danger, and to protect the country and our fellow Marines. The Marines follow all the rules of our nation, along with extra military rules!. So, it is the case that you may be a fully fledged, member of the Marine Corps, and of course, you are still subject to the rules of the nation. That includes Visas and Green Cards!

I heard the news of this investigation, but I did not think this applied to me. After all, I had my Visa, and it was all done the right way. But during this investigation, the discovery was made that my own paperwork was not up to date. I had not kept track of my Visa status, which as it turned out- had a problem. My Visa had expired!

And my smooth road ahead in the US Marines suddenly opened up a gaping hole. I found myself facing deportation back to my country of origin — Panama, on violation of immigration laws. And so, I was informed I would be deported.

No more home! How could this be? No more being able to devote myself to my beloved adopted country that I loved dearly! I could not go back to my family! I was suddenly alone. This was to me a great shock.

I have a sister, her name is Elena. During this time,

she was at work, and she suddenly had a vision that I was in serious trouble. Elena and I had not communicated. There had not even been time for that. I'd been told to immediately pack up, and get ready to be deported. I had not even had a chance to contact my family. No one knew.

But my sister, Elena, she had a vision. It came to her that I was in serious trouble. Elena left work, she went immediately home, and Elena, who is also my Godmother, said ' I must pray for my brother! I know he is in a crisis, it has come to me, through a vision' And so my sister, Elena, my Godmother, began to pray for me. And still she did not even know — I was facing deportation that very same day.

The officer began to load us on the bus to take us for deportation processing.

I was being put on a bus to be deported.

My world had come crashing down.

Suddenly — three names were called out. Three names were spoken. And mine was one. We were told to stand aside from the everyone else. The reason was unknown to us. We stepped aside, as we were told, and we waited.

The officers loaded six out of the seven buses and drove away. We waited, not knowing what would happen next..

I stood at attention, not knowing what would happen, and then the immigration officer approached me. The Immigration Officers can strike fear into your heart, for the Immigration and Naturalization services can determine your future. I realized that all the power I had in the world, could not stand up to what awaited.

Then, the officer handed me an envelope. I looked in the envelope. And there in my hand, was a naturalization number. The officer said to me," You are instructed to New York, and to file for US Citizenship immediately."

To say I was stunned — is an understatement. From thinking my world was crashing down, to my world completely turning around - all happened in an instant!

This did not happen by chance. Who was there behind me, standing above me at my shoulder? It is clear as day and as deep as the night, that this was the Lord. My sister, Elena, saw in her heart I was in trouble, she prayed, and God listened, and God responded on the ' urgent' incoming line!

I thank God for using his faithful servant, the Rev. Elena Bascom - who is both my Godmother, and also my my sister- to deliver me from the devil's path. This was nothing shy of a miracle.

The three Marines who were called to stay back, and instructed to apply for US Citizenship right away- none of us had a valid Visa. We were all in jeopardy. We did not have a work permit much less a green card among the three of us! And in order to become a US Citizen you must first become a resident and maintain your residency or Green Card for 5 years before becoming eligible to citizenship in the United States! That is not what God told the US Marines to do!

God instructed the US Marines to give us a direct path to US citizenship — and not to lose one precious minute!

In a moment of my life, it was the prayers from my sister Pastor Bascom, that put the call in on God's urgent line. The Lord showed me that with Him everything is possible! Even U.S Citizenship!

What a miracle! God is Good, all the time God is Good!

And I know that once a Miracle takes place, it does not say that there will be a second or a third or more Miracles in life! Yet I must let it be known, that God truly acts to bring the power of the positive into the world. There is no greater truth than that God performs Miracles for His Children. God is protecting His Children. God's Miracles do not stop at one.

Protection is a concept that we may think of as here on Earth alone. We have laws and rules, and we are protected by these. But those are human laws, and human rules. There are greater rules that come from the On High. And when you experience that power, you know in your heart of hearts you have been graced by the Almighty.

I talked of my road, earlier, and how it almost was end-of-the road for my home here in the US. And then God intervened. Well, it happened again. My road was going to lead me straight into a jail cell. This is not something a person can think about without imagining a crime has been committed. Your life can be dictated by a mistake - and then you are in need of something to happen. You cannot always correct a mistake on your own.

It can take God to set the record straight. It can take a Miracle.

And here is what happened. I was working for the US Postal Service; when I was no longer an active US Marine. I had purchased a 35" TV and two VCRs from an acquaintance. However, the items obtained by my acquaintance, it turned out were purchased from Circuit City with stolen credit cards. During the investigation, the police discovered that I had been one of the purchasers from my acquaintance, of several items - the TV and VCRs. Therefore, they decided I was to be charged with possession of stolen property, and conspiracy.

I was arrested, and I taken to the police. I was charged, and there was a court date set. They did not throw me behind bars then. I was allowed out on my own recognizance. After I was let go at the police station, the first person I called was my Pastor, who is my Godmother and also my sister! The Rev. Bascom without excitation, right away began to pray on my behalf every single day, as the date of my trial approached. She and God wasted no time!

On court day, the Judge began by reading out loud the charges against me, but prior to that there were three other cases on the docket on that day, and the judge sentenced them all to maximum time in prison. Naturally, I was worried! I heard those sentences and I thought, "This is what is in store for me, too." But I followed the instructions given to me by my sister, Rev. Bascom, and so, I began repeating Psalm 91 over and over and over until it was my turn to see the judge.

As I stood in front of the judge, he suddenly began coughing uncontrollably each time he tried to pass sentence on me. After, a minute the Judge ask the lawyer to approach the bench.Next the lawyer returned to his seat and started gathering his papers and looked at me and said, "let us go". (I thought that may sentencing had been postponed) However, as I walked outside with the lawyer he said " I'm not sure what happened but the charges against you have been dropped, just return the items. There is no further judgment the court will pass. You are not being convicted or sentenced, you are free to go.

My eyes widened, my mouth dropped wide open. I ran to a private place in the courthouse, and I began to praise God for His mercy and blessing over me!

I went home and called my sister and we began to praise God for yet another miracle in my life.

God is good, all the time God is good! How can we not praise Him!

How is it that God watches over His Children so dearly and carefully? My sister, the Rev. Bascom, knows that when God is needed, He is there. And I have felt the power of the Lord, I know the channel to the Lord is wide and it is ever-present. He hears his Children, and he steps in when the time is one of pain and anguish. These moments are Miracles.

Are you ready for more? It is the case that there are many

Miracles in life.

How is it so? It is so because the Lord on High is here, all the time, in your life.

During a very painful divorce, I was self-destructing, missing work for days in a row, walking for miles with no destination, depressed, angry, lost, and alone. I had decided that the only thing left for me to do was to end my life. I set out to do just that by causing an accident with another vehicle at a high rate of speed in hopes of ending my life. As I drove through the city recklessly while speeding through red lights, there was a pay phone at a supermarket and for some reason I stopped to use the pay phone to call my Pastor Bascom, who is also my sister and my Godmother. I called her one last time to say "Thank you for everything and for caring enough to bring me out of Panama where we grew up in poverty."

The second my sister answered the phone, she sensed that something was wrong with me and began to probe and pray with me. Before you know it, I was on the phone with my sister for over 4 hours and by the time we were done, I had no more desire to kill myself. God used my Pastor/Godmother/Sister to save my life and show me a better way.

All I had to do was to believe that *"God so loved the world, that he gave his only begotten Son, that whosoever believeth in him should not perish, but have everlasting life." (John 3:16)*

Life has a way of pushing you forward, and does not stay still! Even if you think you want to just 'stop,' and you go at high speed trying to outrun life itself - this is not the way forward.

After I stopped my self-destructive behavior, and my Rev. Bascom prayed for me to help me to come to a halt on that downward slope, I looked at life and reazlied it was time for me to obtain a better education. I had stopped at the 11th grade. I did not finish High School.

One morning after having breakfast, I decided it was time for me to obtain a not just my high school diploma, but to look higher. I decided I would go for otaining a graduate degree. However, this seemed insurmountable. I knew it was my heart's desire to go farther in my education. But I'd made mistakes in the past. It wasn't just that I had not valued an education. It was that I had not put a large enough value on my own life, on who I was, and what I could do.

I turned to Rev Bascom, and I asked for prayer. Could I go farther in my education? I asked for the Lord's help to overcome obstacles. I knew there would be challenges, but I committed to my education, and to being devoted to God.

When you devote yourself unconditionally to our Lord, you bring yourself through prayer to your own higher powers, too. And there are pathways to grace that you do not open up by yourself. These are opened through the power of the Lord.

Today, by the grace of God I hold four Masters, a doctorate in Information Technology and another doctorate in Logistics and Supply Chain Management. This is where I have found my best self, through my education, even though it was without early obtaining a High School Diploma or my Bachelors.

God is good, all the time God is good!

The past few years have been changes that all of us could hardly have imagined. We know that there are ups and downs in life. When you are in a down period, you cannot imagine this will change. It can feel like you are pushed down, and you cannot even raise your body up and hold it up during the day. In 2019, I could not hold my head up without pain and migraines. It was necessary for me to have Posterior Cervical Laminectomy and Fusion of the C4-C5, C5-C6, C6-C7 vertebrates.

This procedure was extremely painful after surgery and I was unable to move or help myself in any way, for over 7 days. One morning the doctor came in and said, "the hospital needs the bed and you have been here for a week." Today, health care has a very high need for the beds, as we all know. He said, ' I am sorry but we have to transfer you to another location.'

He decided to release me over to a stay in physical therapy clinic for 30 days. At that time, my Rev. Bascom, was not nearby. She was not in the country at the time of my surgery. She was far away, in Panama at the time of my surgery. Yet, she sensed there was something wrong. Out fo the blue, she called me. I told her that the following morning I was being move to a clinic for 30 days. I knew, and frankly my doctor knew, too, that this was not the ideal. In fact, I was still very weak and in pain. This could go either way. The therapy clinic might actually cause me harm if it was too soon to be there, the conditions would not be right. In fact, I knew that this transfer was dangerous to my recovery. When you are in a hospital and you are told you have to leave -- if you are in pain, and dependent upon help -- you can go downhill if you are moved.

Rev. Bascom heard my situation. And she prayed for me. At this time she also prayed to the Virgin Mary and asked her to help me.

Until that time, every day after the surgery I had not been able to stand, to walk, to do anything for myself. I was dependent on the nurses. But that next morning I was able to get out of bed and walked to the bathroom by myself. By 3pm I discharged from the hospital. However, instead of heading to another clinic I went home.

God is good, all the time God is good.

During my life there have been so many blessing/miracles giving by God. So, knowing where I came from to where I am today is nothing short from a Miracle! God helped me achieve the highest enlisted rank in the US Military "Command Sergeant Major" in charge of the Pacific from Alaska to Australia. I was instrumental in the reopening of Pearl Harbor for the locals to visit and in the construction of pipelines and railhead from Alaska into Canada. I received numerous honors during my military career.

Here are a few that would not be possible but by the grace of God.

I was presented with the Commander-In-Chief golden coin from President Bill Clinton during Operation Restore Hope, and for my service in Bosnia and Herzegovina.

I received The Commander in Chief's Installation of Excellence Award from President Barack Hussein Obama and Vice President Joseph Robinette Biden during the 25th annual military awards ceremony in Washington, D.C.

Throughout my military career God never stopped blessing me from Somalia, Bosnia, Kosovo, and the Gaza Stirp in Tel Aviv Israel, to Iraq, and Afghanistan He brought me out without a scratch.

I retired after 27 years of military service with the following medals: the Legion of Merit, two Bronze Star, five Meritorious Service Medal, and two Defense Meritorious Service Medals.

Now you have heard about my life, and just a few of God's many blessings.